Mr. Bonaparte of
CORSICA

John Kendrick Bangs

1st WORLD
LIBRARY
Literary Society

Mr. Bonaparte of Corsica

John Kendrick Bangs

© 1st World Library – Literary Society, 2005
PO Box 2211
Fairfield, IA 52556
www.1stworldlibrary.org
First Edition

LCCN: 2006902740

Softcover ISBN: 1-4218-1870-1
Hardcover ISBN: 1-4218-1770-5
eBook ISBN: 1-4218-1970-8

Purchase *"Mr. Bonaparte of Corsica"*
as a traditional bound book at:
www.1stWorldLibrary.org/purchase.asp?ISBN=1-4218-1870-1

1st World Library Literary Society is a nonprofit
organization dedicated to promoting literacy by:

- Creating a free internet library accessible from any
computer worldwide.
- Hosting writing competitions and offering book
publishing scholarships.

Readers interested in supporting literacy
through sponsorship, donations or
membership please contact:
literacy@1stworldlibrary.org
Check us out at: www.1stworldlibrary.ORG
and start downloading free ebooks today.

Mr. Bonaparte of Corsica
contributed by Tim, Ed & Rodney
in support of
1st World Library Literary Society

CONTENTS

I. CORSICA TO BRIENNE 1769-1779 7

II. BRIENNE 1779-1785 14

III. PARIS - VALENCE - LYONS - CORSICA 1785-1793 ... 23

IV. SARDINIA - TOULON - NICE - PARIS - BARRAS -
    JOSEPHINE 1793-1796 31

V. ITALY - MILAN - VIENNA - VENICE 1796-1797 41

VI. MONTEBELLO - PARIS - EGYPT 1797-1799 51

VII. THE 19TH BRUMAIRE - CONSUL -
     THE TUILERIES - CAROLINE 1799 63

VIII. THE ALPS - THE EMPIRE -
      THE CORONATION 1800-1804 71

IX. THE RISE OF THE EMPIRE 1805-1810 79

X. THE FALL OF THE EMPIRE 1810-1814 89

XI. A ELBA - THE RETURN - WATERLOO -
    ST. HELENA 1814-1815 99

XII. 1815-1821-1895 109

CHAPTER I

CORSICA TO BRIENNE 1769-1779

Napoleon's father, Charles Bonaparte, was the honored progenitor of thirteen children, of whom the man who subsequently became the Emperor of the French, by some curious provision of fate, was the second. That the infant Napoleon should have followed rather than led the procession is so foreign to the nature of the man that many worthy persons unfamiliar with the true facts of history have believed that Joseph was a purely apocryphal infant, or, as some have suggested, merely an adopted child; but that Napoleon did upon this occasion content himself with second place is an incontrovertible fact. Nor is it entirely unaccountable. It is hardly to be supposed that a true military genius, such as Napoleon is universally conceded to have been, would plunge into the midst of a great battle without first having acquainted himself with the possibilities of the future. A reconnoitre of the field of action is the first duty of a successful commander; and hence it was that Napoleon, not wishing to rush wholly unprepared into the battle of life, assigned to his brother Joseph the arduous task of first entering into the world to see how the land lay. Joseph having found everything to his satisfaction, Napoleon made his appearance in the little island of Corsica, recently come under French domination the 15th day August, 1769. Had he been born two months earlier, we are told, he would have been an Italian. Had he been born a hundred years later, it is difficult to say what he would have been. As it was, he was born a Frenchman. It is not pleasant to contemplate what the man's future would have been had he been born an Italian, nor is it easy to picture that future with any confidence born of certainty. Since the days of Caesar, Italy had not produced any great military commander, and it is not likely that the powers would have changed their scheme, confirmed by sixteen centuries of observance, in Napoleon's behalf - a fact which Napoleon himself realized, for he often said in his latter days, with a shudder: "I hate to think how inglorious I should have become had I been born two months earlier and entered the world as an Italian. I should have been another Joseph - not that Joseph is not a good man, but he is not a great man. Ah! Bourrienne, we cannot be too careful in the selection of our birthdays."

It is the testimony of all who knew him in his infancy that Napoleon was a good child. He was obedient and respectful to his mother, and sometimes at night when, on account of some indigestible quality of his food or other cause, it was necessary for his father to make a series of forced marches up and down the spacious nursery in the beautiful home at Ajaccio, holding the infant warrior in his arms, certain premonitions of his son's future career dawned upon the parent. His anguish was voiced in commanding tones; his wails, like his subsequent addresses to his soldiers, were short, sharp, clear, and decisive, nor would he brook the slightest halt in these midnight marches until the difficulties which stood in his path had been overcome. His confidence in himself at this early period was remarkable. Quick to make up his mind, he was tenacious of his purpose to the very end.

It is related that when barely seven months old, while sitting in his nurse's lap, by means of signs which she could not fail to comprehend, he expressed the desire, which, indeed, is characteristic of most healthy Children of that age, to possess the whole of the outside world, not to mention the moon and other celestial bodies. Reaching his little hands out in the direction of the Continent, lying not far distant over the waters of the Mediterranean, he made this demand; and while, of course, his desire was not granted upon the instant, it is the testimony of history that he never lost sight of that cherished object.

After providing Napoleon with eleven other brothers and sisters, Charles Bonaparte died, and left his good and faithful wife Letitia to care for the future greatness of his family, a task rendered somewhat the more arduous than it might otherwise have been by the lack of income; but the good woman, who had much of Napoleon's nature in her make-up, was equal to the occasion. She had her sons to help her, and was constantly buoyed up by the expressed determination of her second child to place her beyond the reach of want in that future day when the whole world lay grovelling at his feet.

"Do not worry, mother," Napoleon said. "Let Joseph and Lucien and Louis and Jerome and the girls be educated; as for me, I can take care of myself. I, who at the age of three have mastered the Italian language, have a future before me. I will go to France, and then -"

"Well! what then?" his mother asked.

"Nous verrons!" Napoleon replied, turning on his heel and walking out of the house whistling a military march.

From this it will be seen that even in his in fancy Napoleon had his ideas as to his future course. Another anecdote, which is taken from the unpublished memoirs of the grandson of one of his Corsican nurses, illustrates in an equally vivid manner how, while a mere infant in arms, he had a passion for and a knowledge of military terms. Early one morning the silence was broken by the incipient Emperor calling loudly for assistance. His nurse, rushing to him, discovered that the point of a pin was sticking into his back. Hastily removing the cause of the disturbance, she endeavored to comfort him:

"Never mind, sweetheart," she said, "it's only a nasty pin."

"Nasty pin!" roared Napoleon. "By the revered name of Paoli,

I swear I thought it was a bayonet!"

It was, no doubt, this early realization of the conspicuous part he was to play in the history of his time that made the youthful Bonaparte reserved of manner, gloomy, and taciturn, and prone to irritability. He felt within him the germ of future greatness, and so became impatient of restraint. He completely dominated the household. Joseph, his elder brother, became entirely subject to the imperious will of the future Emperor; and when in fancy Napoleon dreamed of those battles to come, Joseph was always summoned to take an active part in the imaginary fight. Now he was the bridge of Lodi, and, lying flat on his back, was forced to permit his bloodthirsty brother to gallop across him, shouting words of inspiration to a band of imaginary followers; again he was forced to pose as a snow-clad Alp for Napoleon to climb, followed laboriously by Lucien and Jerome and the other children. It cannot be supposed that this was always pleasing to Joseph, but he never faltered when the demand was made that he should act, because he did not dare.

"You bring up the girls, mother," Napoleon had said. "Leave the boys to me and I'll make kings of them all, if I have to send them over to the United States, where all men will soon be potentates, and their rulers merely servants - chosen to do their bidding."

Once, Joseph venturing to assert himself as the eldest son, Napoleon smiled grimly.

"And what, pray, does that mean?" he asked, scornfully.

"That I and not you am the head of the family," replied Joseph.

"Very well," said Napoleon, rushing behind him, and, by a rapidly conceived flank movement, giving Joseph a good sound kick. "How does the head of the family like the foot of the family? Don't ever prate of accidents of birth to me."

From that time on Joseph never murmured again, but obeyed blindly his brother's slightest behest. He would have permitted Napoleon to mow him down with grape-shot without complaint rather than rebel and incur the wrath which he knew would then fall upon his head.

At school the same defiance of restraint and contempt for superior strength characterized Napoleon. Here, too, his taciturn nature helped him much. If he were asked a question which he could not answer, he would decline to speak, so that his instructors were unable to state whether or not he was in ignorance as to the point under discussion, and could mark him down conscientiously as contumelious only. Hence it was that he stood well in his studies, but was never remarkable for deportment. His favorite plaything, barring his brother Joseph, was a small brass cannon that weighed some thirty odd pounds, and which is still to be seen on the island of Corsica. Of this he once said: "I'd rather hear its report than listen to a German band; though if I could get them both playing at the same time there'd be one German band less in the world."

This remark found its parallel later on when, placed by Barras in command of the defenders of the Convention against the attacks of the Sectionists, Napoleon was asked the chairman of the Assembly to send them occasional reports as to how matters progressed. His reply was terse.

"Legislators," he said, "you ask me for an occasional report. If you listen you will hear the report of my cannon. That is all you'll get, and it will be all you need. I am here. I will save you."

"It is a poor time for jokes," said a representative.

"It is a worse time for paper reports," retorted Napoleon. "It would take me longer to write out a legislative report than it will to clean out the mob. Besides, I want it understood at this end of my career that autograph-hunters are going to get left."

As he turned, Barras asked him as to his intentions.

"Where are you going?" he asked.

"To make a noise in the world," cried Napoleon; "au revoir."

That he had implanted in him the essential elements of a great fighter his school-companions were not long in finding out.

When not more than five years of age he fell in love with a little schoolmate, and, being jeered at for his openly avowed sentiments, he threatened to thrash the whole school, adding to the little maiden that he would thrash her as well unless she returned his love, a line of argument which completely won her heart, particularly in view of the fact that he proved his sincerity by fulfilling that part of his assumed obligations which referred to the subjugation of the rest of the school. It was upon this occasion that in reference to his carelessness of dress, his schoolmates composed the rhyme,

> "Napoleon di mezza calzetta
> Fa l'amore a Giacominetta."

which, liberally translated, means,

> "Hi! Look at Nap! His socks down of his shin,
> Is making love to little Giacomin."

To this Napoleon, on the authority of the Memoirs of his Father's Hired Man, retorted:

> "I would advise you, be not indiscreet,
> Or I will yank YOUR socks right of your feet."

All of which goes to show that at no time in his youth was he to be trifled with. In poetry or a pitched battle he was quite equal to any emergency, and his companions were not long in finding it out.

John Kendrick Bangs

So passed the infancy of Mr. Bonaparte, of Corsica. It was, after all, much like the extreme youth of most other children. In everything he undertook he was facile princeps, and in nothing that he said or did is there evidence that he failed to appreciate what lay before him. A visitor to the family once ventured the remark, "I am sorry, Napoleon, for you little Corsicans. You have no Fourth of July or Guy Fawkes Day to celebrate."

"Oh, as for that," said Napoleon, "I for one do not mind. I will make national holidays when I get to be a man, and at present I can get along without them. What's the use of Fourth of July when you can shoot off fireworks everyday?"

It was a pertinent question, the visitor departed much impressed with the boy's precocity, which was rendered doubly memorable by Napoleon's humor in discharging fifteen pounds of wadding from his cannon into the visitor's back as he went out of the front gate.

At the age of six Napoleon put aside all infantile pleasures, and at eight assumed all the dignity of that age. He announced his intention to cease playing war with his brother Joseph.

"I am no longer a child, Joseph," he said; "I shall no longer thrash you in play. Here-after I shall do it in sober earnest."

Which no doubt is why, in 1779, Napoleon having stuck faithfully to his promise, Joseph heartily seconded his younger brother's demand that he should leave Corsica and take a course of military instruction at Brienne.

"I shall no doubt miss my dear brother Napoleon," Joseph said to his mother; "but I would not stand in the way of his advancement. Let him go, even though by his departure I am deprived of all opportunity to assist him in his pleasing games of war."

CHAPTER II

BRIENNE 1779-1785

As we have seen, the young Corsican was only ten years of age when, through the influence of Count Marboeuf, an old friend of the Bonaparte family, he was admitted to the military school at Brienne. Those who were present at the hour of his departure from home say that Napoleon would have wept like any other child had he yielded to the impulses of his heart, and had he not detected a smile of satisfaction upon the lips of his brother Joseph. It was this smile that drove all tender emotions from his breast. Taking Joseph to one side, he requested to know the cause of his mirth.

"I was thinking of something funny," said Joseph, paling slightly as he observed the stern expression of Napoleon's face.

"Oh, indeed," said Napoleon; "and what was that something? I'd like to smile myself."

"H'm! - ah - why," faltered Joseph, "it may not strike you as funny, you know. What is a joke for one man is apt to be a serious matter for another, particularly when that other is of a taciturn and irritable disposition."

"Very likely," said Napoleon, dryly; "and sometimes what is a joke for the man of mirth is likewise in the end a serious matter for that same humorous person. This may turn out to be the case in the present emergency. What was the joke? If I do not find it a humorous joke, I'll give you a parting caress which you won't forget in a hurry."

"I was only thinking," said Joseph, uneasily, "that it is a very good thing for that little ferry-boat you are going away on that you are going on it."

Here Joseph smiled weakly, but Napoleon was grim as ever.

"Well," he said, impatiently, "what of that?"

"Why," returned Joseph, "it seemed to me that such a tireless little worker as the boat is would find it very restful to take a Nap."

For an instant Napoleon was silent.

"Joseph," said he, as he gazed solemnly out of the window, "I thank you from the bottom of my heart for this. I had had regrets at leaving home. A moment ago I was ready to break down for the sorrow of parting from my favorite Alp, from my home, from my mother, and my little brass cannon; but now - now I can go with a heart steeled against emotion. If you are going in for humor of that kind, I'm glad I'm going away. Farewell."

With this, picking Joseph up in his arms and concealing him beneath the sofa cushions, Napoleon imprinted a kiss upon his mother's cheek, rushed aboard the craft that was to bear him to fame, and was soon but a memory in the little house at Ajaccio. "Parting is such sweet sorrow," murmured Joseph, as he watched the little vessel bounding over the turquoise waters of the imprisoned sea. "I shall miss him; but there are those who wax fat on grief, and, if I know myself, I am of that brand."

Arrived at Paris, Napoleon was naturally awe-stricken by the splendors of that wonderful city.

"I shall never forget the first sight I had of Paris," he said, years later, when speaking of his boyhood to Madame Junot, with whom he was enjoying a tete-a-tete in the palace at Versailles. "I wondered if I hadn't died of sea-sickness on the way over, as I had several times wished I might, and got to heaven. I didn't know how like the other place it was at that time, you see. It was like an enchanted land, a World's Fair forever, and the prices I had to pay for things quite carried out the World's Fair idea. They were enormous. Weary with walking, for instance, I hired a fiacre and drove about the city for an hour, and it cost me fifty francs; but I fell in with pleasant enough people, one of whom gave me a ten-franc ticket entitling me to a seat on a park bench - for five francs."

Madame Junot laughed.

"And yet they claim that bunco is a purely American institution," she said.

"Dame!" cried Napoleon, rising from the throne, and walking excitedly up and down the palace floor, "I never realized until this moment that I had been swindled! Bourrienne, send Fouche to me. I remember the man distinctly, and if he lives he has yet to die."

Calming down, he walked to Madame Junot's side, and, taking her by the hand, continued:

"And then the theatres! What revelations of delight they were! I used to go to the Theatre Francais whenever I could sneak away and had the money to seat me with the gods in the galleries. Bernhardt was then playing juvenile parts, and Coquelin had not been heard of. Ah! my dear Madame Junot," he added, giving her ear a delicate pinch, "those were the days when life seemed worth the living - when one of a taciturn nature and prone to irritability could find real pleasure in existence. Oh to be unknown again!"

And then, Madame Junot's husband having entered the room,

the Emperor once more relapsed into a moody silence.

But to return to Brienne. Napoleon soon found that there is a gulf measurable by no calculable distance between existence as the dominating force of a family and life as a new boy at a boarding-school. He found his position reversed, and he began for the first time in his life to appreciate the virtues of his brother Joseph. He who had been the victorious general crossing the Alps now found himself the Alp, with a dozen victorious generals crossing him; he who had been the gunner was now the target, and his present inability to express his feelings in language which his tormentors could understand, for he had not yet mastered the French tongue, kept him in a state of being which may well be termed volcanic.

"I simply raged within in those days," Napoleon once said to Las Casas. "I could have swallowed my food raw and it would have been cooked on its way down, I boiled so. They took me for a snow-clad Alp, when, as a matter of fact, I was a small Vesuvius, with a temperature that would have made Tabasco sauce seem like iced water by contrast."

His treatment at the hands of his fellow-students did much to increase his irritability, but he kept himself well in hand, biding the time when he could repay their insults with interest. They jeered him because he was short - short of stature and short of funds; they twitted him on being an alien, calling him an Italian, and asking him why he did not seek out a position in the street-cleaning bureau instead of endeavoring to associate with gentlemen. To this the boy made a spirited reply.

"I am fitting myself for that," he said. "I'll sweep your Parisian streets some day, and some of you particles will go with the rest of the dust before my broom."

He little guessed how prophetic were these words.

Again, they tormented Napoleon on being the son of a lawyer, and asked him who his tailor was, and whether or not his garments were the lost suits of his father's clients, the result of which was that, though born of an aristocratic family, the boy became a pronounced Republican, and swore eternal enmity to the high-born. Another result of this attitude towards him was that he retired from the companionship of all save his books, and he became intimate with Homer and Ossian and Plutarch - familiar with the rise and fall of emperors and empires. Challenged to fight a duel with one of his classmates for a supposititious insult, he accepted, and, having the choice in weapons, chose an examination in mathematics, the one first failing in a demonstration to blow his brains out. "That is the safer for you," he said to his adversary. "You are sure to lose; but the after-effects will not be fatal, because you have no brains to blow out, so you can blow out a candle instead."

Whatever came of the duel we are not informed; but it is to be presumed that it did not result fatally for young Bonaparte, for he lived many years after the incident, as most of our readers are probably aware. Had he not done so, this biography would have had to stop here, and countless readers of our own day would have been deprived of much entertaining fiction that is even now being scattered broadcast over the world with Napoleon as its hero. His love of books combined with his fondness for military life was never more beautifully expressed than when he wrote to his mother: "With my sword at my side and my Homer in my pocket, I hope to carve my way through the world."

The beauty and simplicity of this statement is not at all affected by Joseph's flippant suggestion that by this Napoleon probably meant that he would read his enemies to sleep with his Homer, and then use his sword to cut their heads off. Joseph, as we have already seen, had been completely subjugated by his younger brother, and it is not to be wondered at, perhaps, that, with his younger brother at a safe distance, he should manifest some jealousy, and affect to treat his sentiments with an unwarranted levity.

For Napoleon's self-imposed solitude everything at Brienne arranged itself propitiously. Each of the students was provided with a small patch of ground which he could do with as he pleased, and Napoleon's use of his allotted share was characteristic. He converted it into a fortified garden, surrounded by trees and palisades.

"Now I can mope in peace," he said - and he did.

It has been supposed by historians that it was here that Napoleon did all of his thinking, mapping out his future career, and some of them have told us what he thought. He dreamed of future glory always, one of them states; but whether upon the authority of a palisade or a tiger-lily is not mentioned. Others have given us his soliloquies as he passed to and fro in this little retreat alone, and heard only by the stars at night; but for ourselves, we must be accurate, and it is due to the reader at this point that we should confess - having no stars in our confidence - our entire ignorance as to what Napoleon Bonaparte said, did, or thought when sitting in solitude in his fortified bower; though if our candid impression is desired we have no hesitation in saying that we believe him to have been in Paris enjoying the sights of the great city during those periods of solitude. Boys are boys in all lands, and a knowledge of that peculiar species of human beings, the boarding-school boy, is convincing that, given a prospect of five or six hours of uninterrupted solitude, no youth of proper spirit would fail to avail himself of the opportunities thus offered to see life, particularly with a city like Paris within easy "hooky" distance.

It must also be remembered that the French had at this time abolished the hereafter, along with the idea of a Deity and all pertaining thereto, so that there was nothing beyond a purely temporal discipline and lack of funds to interfere with Bonaparte's enjoyment of all the pleasures which Paris could give. Of temporal discipline he need have had no fear, since, it was perforce relaxed while he was master of his solitude; as for the lack of funds, history has shown that this never interfered with the fulfilment of Napoleon's hopes, and hence the belief that the beautiful pictures, drawn by historians and painted by masters of the brush, of Napoleon in solitude should be revised to include a few accessories, drawn from such portions of Parisian life as will readily suggest themselves.

In his studies, however, Napoleon ranked high. His mathematical abilities were so marked that it was stated that he could square the circle with his eyes closed and both hands tied behind his back.

"The only circle I could not square at that time," said he, "was the family circle, being insufficiently provided with income to do so. I might have succeeded better had not Joseph's appetite grown too fast for the strength of my pocket; that was the only respect, however, in which I ever had any difficulty in keeping up with my dear elder brother." It was here, too, that he learned the inestimably important military fact that the shortest distance between two points is in a straight line; and that he had fully mastered that fact was often painfully evident to such of his schoolmates as seemed to force him to measure with his right arm the distance between his shoulder and the ends of their noses. Nor was he utterly without wit. Asked by a cribbing comrade in examination what a corollary was, Napoleon scornfully whispered back:

"A mathematical camel with two humps."

In German only was he deficient, much to the irritation of his instructor.

"Will you ever learn anything?" asked M. Bouer, the German teacher.

"Certainly," said Napoleon; "but no more German. I know the only word I need in that language."

"And what, pray, is that?"

"Surrender; that's all I'll ever wish to say to the Germans. But lest I get it wrong, pray tell me the imperative form of surrender in your native tongue."

M. Bouer's reply is not known to history, but it was probably not one which the Master of Etiquette at Brienne could have entirely commended.

So he lived at Brienne, thoroughly mastering the science of war; acquiring a military spirit; making no friends, but commanding ultimately the fearsome respect of his school-mates. One or two private interviews with little aristocrats who jeered at him for his ancestry convinced them that while he might not have had illustrious ancestors, it was not unlikely that he would in time develop illustrious descendants, and the jeerings and sneerings soon ceased. The climax of Bonaparte's career at Brienne was in 1784, when he directed a snowball fight between two evenly divided branches of the school with such effect that one boy had his skull cracked and the rest were laid up for weeks from their wounds.

"It was a wonderful fight," remarked Napoleon, during his campaign in Egypt. "I took good care that an occasional missent ball should bowl off the hat of M. Bouer, and whenever any particularly aristocratic aristocrat's head showed itself above the ramparts, an avalanche fell upon his facade with a dull, sickening thud. I have never seen an American college football game, but from all I can learn from accounts in the Paris editions of the American newspapers the effects physical in our fight and that game are about the same."

In 1784, shortly after this episode, Napoleon left Brienne, having learned all that those in authority there could teach him, and in 1785 he applied for and received admission to the regular army, much to the relief of Joseph.

"If he had flunked and come back to Corsica to live," said Joseph, "I think I should have emigrated. I love him dearly, but I'm fonder of myself, and Corsica, large as it is, is too small to contain Napoleon Bonaparte and his brother Joseph simultaneously, particularly as Joseph is distinctly weary of being used as an understudy for a gory battle-field."

CHAPTER III

PARIS - VALENCE - LYONS - CORSICA 1785-1793

The feeling among the larger boys at Brienne at Napoleon's departure was much the same as that experienced by Joseph when his soon to-be-famous brother departed from Corsica. The smaller boys regretted his departure, since it had been one of their greatest pleasures to watch Napoleon disciplining the upper classmen, but Bonaparte was as glad to go as the elders were to have him.

"Brienne is good enough in its way," said he; "but what's the use of fighting children? It's merely a waste of time cracking a youngster's skull with a snowball when you can go out into the real world and let daylight into a man's whole system with a few ounces of grape-shot."

He had watched developments at Paris, too, with the keenest interest, and was sufficiently far-seeing to know that the troubles of the King and Queen and their aristocratic friends boded well for a man fond of a military life who had sense enough to be on the right side. That it took an abnormal degree of intelligence to know which was the right side in those troublous days he also realized, and hence he cultivated that taciturnity and proneness to irritability which we have already mentioned.

"If it had not been for my taciturnity, Talleyrand," he observed, when in the height of his power, "I should have got it in the neck."

"Got what in the neck?" asked Talleyrand.

"The guillotine," rejoined the Emperor. "It was the freedom of speech which people of those sanguinary days allowed themselves that landed many a fine head in the basket. As for me, I simply held my tongue with both hands, and when I wearied of that I called some one in to hold it for me. If I had filled the newspapers with 'Interviews with Napoleon Bonaparte,' and articles on 'Where is France at?' with monographs in the leading reviews every month on 'Why I am what I am,' and all such stuff as that, I'd have condensed my career into one or two years, and ended by having my head divorced from my shoulders in a most commonplace fashion. Taciturnity is a big thing when you know how to work it, and so is proneness to irritability. The latter keeps you from making friends, and I didn't want any friends just then. They were luxuries which I couldn't afford. You have to lend money to friends; you have to give them dinners and cigars, and send bonbons to their sisters. A friend in those days would have meant bankruptcy of the worst sort. Furthermore, friends embarrass you when you get into public office, and try to make you conspicuous when you'd infinitely prefer to saw wood and say nothing. I took my loneliness straight, and that is one of the reasons why I am now the Emperor of France, and your master."

Before entering the army a year at a Parisian military school kept Bonaparte busy. There, as at Brienne, he made his influence felt. He found his fellow-pupils at Paris living in a state of luxury that was not in accord with his ideas as to what a soldier should have. Whether or not his new school-mates, after the time-honored custom, tossed him in a blanket on the first night of his arrival, history does not say, but Bonaparte had hardly been at the school a week when he complained to the authorities that there was too much luxury in their system for him.

"Cadets do not need feather-beds and eider-down quilts," he said; "and as for the sumptuous viands we have served at mealtime, they are utterly inappropriate. I'd rather have a plate of Boston baked beans or steaming buckwheat cakes to put my mind into that state which should characterize the thinking apparatus of a soldier than a dozen of the bouchees financieres and lobster Newburgs and other made-dishes which you have on your menu. Made-dishes and delicate beverages make one mellow and genial of disposition. What we need is the kind of food that will destroy our amiability and put us in a frame of mind calculated to make willing to kill our best friends - nay, our own brothers and sisters - if occasion arises, with a smiling face. Look at me. I could kill my brother Joseph, dear as he is to me, and never shed a tear, and it's buckwheat-cakes and waffles that have done it!"

Likewise he abhorred dancing.

"Away with dancing men!" he cried, impatiently, at one time when in the height of his power, to his Minister of War. "Suppose when I was crossing the Alps my soldiers had been of your dancing sort. How far would I have got if every time the band played a two-step my grenadiers had dropped their guns to pirouette over those snow-white wastes? Let the diplomats do the dancing. For soldiers give me men to whom the polka is a closed book and the waltz an abomination."

Holding these views, he naturally failed to win the sympathy of his fellows at the Paris school who, young nobles for the most part, could not understand his point of view. So, having nothing else to do, he applied himself solely to his studies and to reflection, and it was the happiest moment of his life up to that time when, having passed his examinations for entrance to the regular army, he received his commission as a second lieutenant.

"Now we're off!" he said to himself, as he surveyed himself in the mirror, after donning his uniform.

"It does not set very well in the back," remarked one of the maids of the pension in which he lived, glancing in at the door.

"It does not matter," returned Bonaparte, loftily. "As long as it sets well in front I'm satisfied; for you should know, madame, that a true soldier never shows his back, and that is the kind of a military person I am. A false front would do for me. I am no tin soldier, which in after-years it will interest you to remember. When you are writing your memoirs this will make an interesting anecdote."

From this it is to be inferred that at this time he had no thought of Moscow. Immediately after his appointment Bonaparte repaired to Valence, where his regiment was stationed and where he formed a strong attachment for the young daughter of Madame du Colombier, with whom, history records, he ate cherries before breakfast. This was his sole dissipation at that time, but his felicity was soon to be interrupted. His regiment was ordered to Lyons, and Bonaparte and his love were parted.

"Duty calls me, my dear," he said, on leaving her. "I would stay if I could, but I can't, and, on the whole, it is just as well. If I stayed I should marry you, and that would never do. You cannot support me, nor I you. We cannot live on cherries, and as yet my allowance is an ingrowing one - which is to say that it goes from me to my parent, and not from my parent to me. Therefore, my only love, farewell. Marry some one else. There are plenty of men who are fond of cherries before breakfast, and there is no reason why one so attractive as you should not find a lover."

The unhappy girl was silent for a moment. Then, with an ill-suppressed sob, she bade him go.

"You are right, Napoleon," she said. "Go. Go where duty calls you, and if you get tired of Lyons -"

John Kendrick Bangs

"Yes?" he interrupted, eagerly.

"Try leopards!" she cried, rushing from his embrace into the house.

Bonaparte never forgave this exhibition of flippancy, though many years after, when he learned that his former love, who had married, as he had bade her do, and suffered, was face to face with starvation, it is said, on the authority of one of his ex-valet's memoirs, that he sent her a box of candied cherries from one of the most expensive confectionery-shops of Paris.

After a brief sojourn at Lyons, Napoleon was summoned with his regiment to quell certain popular tumults at Auxonne. There he distinguished himself as a handler of mobs, and learned a few things that were of inestimable advantage to him later. Speaking of it in after-years, he observed: "It is my opinion, my dear Emperor Joseph, that grape-shot is the only proper medicine for a mob. Some people prefer to turn the hose on them, but none of that for me. They fear water as they do death, but they get over water. Death is more permanent. I've seen many a rioter, made respectable by a good soaking, return to the fray after he had dried out, but in all my experience I have never known a man who was once punctured by a discharge of grape-shot who took any further interest in rioting."

About this time he began to regulate his taciturnity. On occasions he had opinions which he expressed most forcibly. In 1790, having gone to an evening reception at Madame Neckar's, he electrified his hostess and her guests by making a speech of some five hundred words in length, too long to be quoted here in full, but so full of import and delivered with such an air of authority that La Fayette, who was present, paled visibly, and Mirabeau, drawing Madame de Stael to one side, whispered, trembling with emotion, "Who is that young person?"

Whether this newly acquired tendency to break in upon the

reserve which had hitherto been the salient feature of his speech had anything to do with it or not we are not aware, but shortly afterwards Napoleon deemed it wise to leave his regiment for a while, and to return to his Corsican home on furlough. Of course an affecting scene was enacted by himself and his family when they were at last reunited. Letitia, his fond mother, wept tears of joy, and Joseph, shaking him by the hand, rushed, overcome with emotion, from the house. Napoleon shortly after found him weeping in the garden.

"Why so sad, Joseph?" he inquired. "Are you sorry I have returned?"

"No, dear Napoleon," said Joseph, turning away his head to hide his tears, "it is not that. I was only weeping because - because, in the nature of things, you will have to go away again, and - the - the idea of parting from you has for the moment upset my equilibrium."

"Then we must proceed to restore it," said Napoleon, and, taking Joseph by the right arm, he twisted it until Joseph said that he felt quite recovered.

Napoleon's stay at Corsica was quite uneventful. Fearing lest by giving way to love of family, and sitting and talking with them in the luxuriously appointed parlor below-stairs, he should imbibe too strong a love for comfort and ease, and thus weaken his soldierly instincts, as well as break in upon that taciturnity which, as we have seen, was the keynote of his character, he had set apart for himself a small room on the attic floor, where he spent most of his time undisturbed, and at the same time made Joseph somewhat easier in his mind.

"When he's up-stairs I am comparatively safe," said Joseph. "If he stayed below with us I fear I should have a return of my nervous prostration."

Meantime, Napoleon was promoted to a first lieutenancy, and shortly after, during the Reign of Terror in Paris, having once more for the moment yielded to an impulse to speak out in meeting, he denounced anarchy in unmeasured terms, and was arrested and taken to Paris.

"It was a fortunate arrest for me," he said. "There I was in Corsica with barely enough money to pay my way back to the capital. Arrested, the State had to pay my fare, and I got back to active political scenes on a free pass. As for the trial, it was a farce, and I was triumphantly acquitted. The jury was out only fifteen minutes. I had so little to say for myself that the judges began to doubt if I had any ideas on any subject - or, as one of them said, having no head to mention, it would be useless to try and cut it off. Hence my acquittal and my feeling that taciturnity is the mother of safety."

Then came the terrible attack of the mob upon the Tuileries on the 20th of June, 1792. Napoleon was walking in the street with Bourrienne when the attack began.

"There's nothing like a lamp-post for an occasion like this, it broadens one's views so," he said, rapidly climbing up a convenient post, from which he could see all that went on. "I didn't know that this was the royal family's reception-day. Do you want to know what I think?"

"Mumm is the word," whispered Bourrienne. "This is no time to have opinions."

"Mumm may be the word, but water is the beverage. Mumm is too dry. What this crowd needs is a good wetting down," retorted Bonaparte. "If I were Louis XVI. I'd turn the hose on these tramps, and keep them at bay until I could get my little brass cannon loaded. When I had that loaded, I'd let them have a few balls hot from the bat. This is what comes of being a born king. Louis doesn't know how to talk to the people. He's all right for a state-dinner, but when it comes to a mass-meeting he is not in it."

And then as the King, to gratify the mob, put the red cap of

Jacobinism upon his head, the man who was destined before many years to occupy the throne of France let fall an ejaculation of wrath.

"The wretches!" he cried. "How little they know! They've only given him another hat to talk through! They'll have to do their work all over again, unless Louis takes my advice and travels abroad for his health."

These words were prophetic, for barely two months later the second and most terrible and portentous attack upon the palace took place - an attack which Napoleon witnessed, as he had witnessed the first, from a convenient lamp-post, and which filled him with disgust and shame; and it was upon that night of riot and bloodshed that he gave utterance to one of his most famous sayings.

"Bourrienne," said he, as with his faithful companions he laboriously climbed the five flights of stairs leading to his humble apartment, "I hate the aristocrats, as you know; and to-day has made me hate the populace as well. What is there left to like?"

"Alas! lieutenant, I cannot say," said Bourrienne, shaking his head sadly.

"What," continued Napoleon, "is the good of anything?"

"I give it up," returned Bourrienne, with a sigh. "I never was good at riddles. What IS the good of anything?"

"Nothing!" said Napoleon, laconically, as he took off his uniform and went to bed.

CHAPTER IV

SARDINIA - TOULON - NICE - PARIS - BARRAS - JOSEPHINE 1793-1796

Greatness now began to dawn for Napoleon. Practically penniless, in a great and heartless city, even the lower classes began to perceive that here was one before whom there lay a brilliant future. Restaurateurs, laundresses, confectioners - all trusted him. An instance of the regard people were beginning to have for him is shown in the pathetic interview between Napoleon and Madame Sans Gene, his laundress.

"Here is your wash, lieutenant," said she, after climbing five flights of stairs, basket in hand, to the miserable lodging of the future Emperor.

Napoleon looked up from his books and counted the clothes.

"There is one sock missing," said he, sternly.

"No," returned Sans Gene. "Half of each sock was washed away, and I sewed the remaining halves into one. One good sock is better than two bad ones. If you ever lose a leg in battle you may find the odd one handy."

"How can I ever repay you?" cried Napoleon, touched by her friendly act.

"I'm sure I don't know," returned Madame Sans Gene,

demurely, "unless you will escort me to the Charity Ball - I'll buy the tickets."

"And, pray, what good will that do?" asked Bonaparte.

"It will make Lefebvre jealous," said Madame Sans Gene, "and maybe that will bring him to the point. I want to marry him, but, encourage him as I will, he does not propose, and as in revising the calendar the government has abolished leap-year, I really don't know what to do."

"I cannot go to the ball," said Napoleon, sadly. "I don't dance, and, besides, I have loaned my dress-suit to Bourrienne. But I will flirt with you on the street if you wish, and perhaps that will suffice."

It is hardly necessary to tell the reader that the ruse was successful, and that Lefebvre, thus brought to the point, married Madame Sans Gene, and subsequently, through his own advancement, made her the Duchess of Dantzig. The anecdote suffices to show how wretchedly poor and yet how full of interest and useful to those about him Napoleon was at the time.

In February, 1793, a change for the better in his fortunes occurred. Bonaparte, in cooperation with Admiral Turget, was ordered to make a descent upon Sardinia. What immediately followed can best be told in Bonaparte's own words. "My descent was all right," he said afterwards, "and I had the Sardines all ready to put in boxes, when Turget had a fit of sea-sickness, lost his bearings, and left me in the lurch. There was nothing left for me but to go back to Corsica and take it out of Joseph, which I did, much to Joseph's unhappiness. It was well for the family that I did so, for hardly had I arrived at Ajaccio when I found my old friend Paoli wrapping Corsica up in a brown-paper bundle to send to the King of England with his compliments. This I resisted, with the result that our whole family was banished, and those fools of Corsicans broke into our house and smashed all of our furniture. They little knew that that furniture, if in existence to-day, would bring millions of francs as curios if sold at auction. It was thus that the family came to move to France and that I became in fact what I had been by birth - a Frenchman. If I had remained a Corsican, Paoli's treachery would have made me an Englishman, to which I should never have become reconciled, although had I been an Englishman I should have taken more real pleasure out of the battle of Waterloo than I got.

"After this I was ordered to Toulon. The French forces here were commanded by General Cartaux, who had learned the science of war painting portraits in Paris. He ought to have been called General Cartoon. He besieged Toulon in a most impressionistic fashion. He'd bombard and bombard and bombard, and then leave the public to guess at the result. It's all well enough to be an impressionist in painting, but when it comes to war the public want more decided effects. When I got there, as a brigadier-general, I saw that Cartaux was wasting his time and ammunition. His idea seemed to be that by firing cannon all day he could so deafen the enemy that at night the French army could sneak into Toulon unheard and capture the city, which was, to say the least, unscientific. I saw at once that Cartaux must go, and I soon managed to make life so unbearable for him that he resigned, and a man named Doppet, a physician, was placed in command. Doppet was worse than Cartaux. Whenever anybody got hurt he'd stop the war and prescribe for the injured man. If he could have prescribed for the enemy they'd have died in greater numbers I have no doubt, but, like the idiot he was, he practised on his own forces. Besides, he was more interested in surgery than in capturing Toulon. He always gave the ambulance corps the right of line, and I believe to this day that his plan of routing the English involved a sudden rush upon them, taking them by surprise, and the subsequent amputation of their legs. The worst feature of the situation, as I found it, was that these two men, falling back upon their rights as my superior officers, refused to take orders from me. I called their attention to the fact that rank had been abolished, and that in France one man was now as good as another; but they were stubborn, so I wrote to Paris and had them removed. Then came Dugommier, who backed me up in my plans, and Toulon as a consequence immediately fell with a dull, sickening thud."

It was during this siege that Bonaparte first encountered Junot. Having occasion to write a note while under fire from the enemy's batteries, Napoleon called for a stenographer. Junot came to him.

"Do you know shorthand?" asked the general, as a bomb exploded at his feet.

"Slightly," said Junot, calmly.

"Take this message," returned the general, coolly, dictating.

Junot took down Bonaparte's words, but just as he finished another bomb exploded near by, scattering dust and earth and sand all over the paper.

"Confounded boors, interrupting a gentleman at his correspondence!" said Bonaparte, with an angry glance at the hostile gunners. "I'll have to dictate that message all over again."

"Yes, general," returned Junot, quickly, "but you needn't mind that. There will be no extra charge. It's really my fault. I should have brought an umbrella."

"You are a noble fellow," said Napoleon, grasping his hand and squeezing it warmly. "In the heyday of my prosperity, if my prosperity ever goes a-haying, I shall remember you. Your name?"

"Junot, General," was the reply.

Bonaparte frowned. "Ha! ha!" he laughed, acridly. "You jest, eh? Well, Junot, when I am Jupiter I'll reward you."

Later on, discovering his error, Bonaparte made a memorandum concerning Junot, which was the first link in the chain which ultimately bound the stenographer to fame as a marshal of France.

There have been various other versions of this anecdote, but this is the only correct one, and is now published for the first time on the authority of M. le Comte de B -, whose grandfather was the bass drummer upon whose drum Junot was writing the now famous letter, and who was afterwards ennobled by Napoleon for his services in Egypt, where, one dark, drizzly night, he frightened away from Bonaparte's tent a fierce band of hungry lions by pounding vigorously upon his instrument.

About this time Napoleon, who had been spelling his name in various ways, and particularly with a "u," as Buonaparte, decided to settle finally upon one form of designation.

"People are beginning to bother the life out of me with requests for my autograph," he said to Bourrienne, "and it is just as well that I should settle on one. If I don't, they'll want me to write out a complete set of them, and I haven't time to do that."

"Buonaparte is a good-looking name," suggested Bourrienne. "It is better than Bona Parte, as you sometimes call yourself. If you settle on Bona Parte, you'd have really three names; and as you don't write society verse for the comic papers, what's the use? Newspaper reporters will refer to you as Napoleon B. Parte or N. Bona Parte, and the public hates a man who parts his name in the middle. Parte is a good name in its way, but it's too short and abrupt. Few men with short, sharp, decisive names like that ever make their mark. Let it be Buonaparte, which is sort of high-sounding - it makes a mouthful, as it were."

"If I drop the 'u' the autograph will be shorter, and I'll gain time writing it," said Napoleon. "It shall be Bonaparte without 'u.'"

"Humph!" ejaculated Bourrienne. "Bonaparte without me! I like that. Might as well talk of Dr. Johnson without Boswell."

Bonaparte now went to Nice as chief of batallion in the army of Italy; but having incurred the displeasure of a suspicious home government, he was shortly superseded, and lived in retirement with his family at Marseilles for a brief time. Here he fell in love again, and would have married Mademoiselle Clery, whom he afterwards made Queen of Sweden, had he not been so wretchedly poor.

"This, my dear," he said, sadly, to Mademoiselle Clery, "is the beastly part of being the original ancestor of a family instead of a descendant. I've got to make the fortune which will enrich posterity, while I'd infinitely prefer having a rich uncle somewhere who'd have the kindness to die and leave me a million. There's Joseph - lucky man. He's gone and got married. He can afford it. He has me to fall back on, but I - I haven't anybody to fall back on, and so, for the second time in my life, must give up the only girl I ever loved."

With these words Napoleon left Mademoiselle Clery, and returned to Paris in search of employment.

"If there's nothing else to do, I can disguise myself as a Chinaman and get employment in Madame Sans Gene's laundry," he said. "There's no disgrace in washing, and in that way I may be able to provide myself with decent linen, anyhow. Then I shall belong to the laundered aristocracy, as the English have it."

But greater things than this awaited Napoleon at Paris. Falling in with Barras, a member of the Convention which ruled France at this time, he learned that the feeling for the restoration of the monarchy was daily growing stronger, and that the royalists of Paris were a great menace to the Convention.

"They'll mob us the first thing we know," said Barras. "The members look to me to save them in case of attack, but I must confess I'd like to sublet the contract."

"Give it to me, then. I'm temporarily out of a job," said Napoleon, "and the life I'm leading is killing me. If it weren't for Talma's kindness in letting me lead his armies on the stage at the Odeon, with a turn at scene-shifting when they are not playing war dramas, I don't know what I'd do for my meals; and even when I do get a sandwich ahead occasionally I have to send it to Marseilles to my mother. Give me your contract, and if I don't save your Convention you needn't pay me a red franc. I hate aristocrats, and I hate mobs; and this being an aristocratic mob, I'll go into the work with enthusiasm."

"You!" cried Barras. "A man of your size, or lack of it, save the Convention from a mob of fifty thousand? Nonsense!"

"Did you ever hear that little slang phrase so much in vogue in America," queried Napoleon, coldly fixing his eye on Barras - "a phrase which in French runs, 'Petit, mais O Moi' - or, as they have it, 'Little, but O My'? Well, that is me. {1} Besides, if I am small, there is less chance of my being killed, which will make me more courageous in the face of fire than one of your bigger men would be."

"I will put my mind on it," said Barras, somewhat won over by Napoleon's self-confidence.

"Thanks," said Napoleon; "and now come into the cafe and have dinner with me."

"Save your money, Bonaparte," said Barras. "You can't afford to pay for your own dinner, much less mine."

"That's precisely why I want you to dine with me," returned Napoleon. "If I go alone, they won't serve me because they know I can't pay. If I go in with you, they'll give me everything they've got on the supposition that you will pay the bill. Come! En avant!"

"Vous etes un bouchonnier, vraiment!" said Barras, with a laugh.

"A what?" asked Napoleon, not familiar with the idiom.

"A corker!" explained Barras.

"Very good," said Napoleon, his face lighting up. "If you'll order a bottle of Burgundy with the bird I will show you that I am likewise something of an uncorker."

This readiness on Napoleon's part in the face of difficulty completely captured Barras, and as a result the young adventurer had his first real chance to make an impression on Paris, where, on the 13th Vendemiaire (or October 4, 1795), he literally obliterated the forces of the Sectionists, whose success in their attack upon the Convention would have meant the restoration of the Bourbons to the throne of France. Placed in command of the defenders of the Convention, Napoleon with his cannon swept the mob from the four broad avenues leading to the palace in which the legislators sat.

"Don't fire over their heads," said he to his gunners, as the mob approached. "Bring our arguments right down to their comprehension, and remember that the comprehension of a royalist is largely affected by his digestion. Therefore, gunners, let them have it there. If these assassins would escape appendicitis they would better avoid the grape I send them."

The result is too well known to need detailed description here. Suffice it to say that Bonaparte's attentions to the digestive apparatus of the rioters were so effective that, in token of their appreciation of his services, the Convention soon afterwards placed him in command of the Army of the Interior.

Holding now the chief military position in Paris, Bonaparte was much courted by every one, but he continued his simple manner of living as of yore, overlooking his laundry and other bills as unostentatiously as when he had been a poor and insignificant subaltern, and daily waxing more taciturn and prone to irritability.

"You are becoming gloomy, General," said Barras one morning, as the two men breakfasted. "It is time for you to marry and become a family man."

"Peste!" said Napoleon, "man of family! It takes too long - it is tedious. Families are delightful when the children are grown up; but I could not endure them in a state of infancy."

"Ah!" smiled Barras, significantly. "But suppose I told you of a place where you could find a family ready made?"

Napoleon at once became interested.

"I should marry it," he said, "for truly I do need some one to look after my clothing, particularly now that, as a man of high rank, my uniforms hold so many buttons."

Thus it happened that Barras took the young hero to a reception at the house of Madame Tallien, where he introduced him to the lovely widow, Josephine de Beauharnais, and her two beautiful children.

"There you are, Bonaparte," he whispered, as they entered the room; "there is the family complete - one wife, one son, one daughter. What more could you want? It will be yours if you ask for it, for Madame de Beauharnais is very much in love with you."

"Ha!" said Napoleon. "How do you know that?"

"She told me so," returned Barras.

"Very well," said Napoleon, making up his mind on the instant. "I will see if I can involve her in a military engagement."

Which, as the world knows, he did; and on the 9th of March, 1796, Napoleon and Josephine were united, and the happy groom, writing to his mother, announcing his marriage to "the only woman he ever loved," said: "She is ten years older than I, but I can soon overcome that. The opportunities for a fast life in Paris are unequalled, and I have an idea that I can catch up with her in six months if the Convention will increase my salary."

John Kendrick Bangs

CHAPTER V

ITALY - MILAN - VIENNA - VENICE 1796-1797

After a honeymoon of ten days Napoleon returned to work. Assuming command of the army of Italy, he said: "I am at last in business for myself. Keep your eyes on me, Bourrienne, and you'll wear blue goggles. You'll have to, you'll be so dazzled. We will set off at once for Italy. The army is in wretched shape. It lacks shoes, clothes, food. It lacks everything. I don't think it even has sense. If it had it would strike for lower wages."

"Lower wages?" queried Bourrienne. "You mean higher, don't you?"

"Not I," said Bonaparte. "They couldn't collect higher wages, but if their pay was reduced they might get it once in a while. We can change all this, however, by invading Italy. Italy has all things to burn, from statuary to Leghorn hats. In three months we shall be at Milan. There we can at least provide ourselves with fine collections of oil-paintings. Meantime let the army feed on hope and wrap themselves in meditation. It's poor stuff, but there's plenty of it, and it's cheap. On holidays give the poor fellows extra rations, and if hope does not sustain them, cheer them up with promises of drink. Tell them when we get to Italy they can drink in the scenery in unstinted measure, and meanwhile keep the band playing merrily. There's nothing like music to drive away hunger. I understand that the lamented king's appetite was seriously affected by the Marseillaise."

To his soldiers he spoke with equal vigor.

"Soldiers," he said, "sartorially speaking, you are a poor lot; but France does not want a tailor-made army at this juncture. We are not about to go on dress parade, but into grim-visaged war, and the patches on your trousers, if you present a bold front to the enemy, need never be seen. You are also hungry, but so am I. I have had no breakfast for four hours. The Republic owes you much; but money is scarce, and you must whistle for your pay. The emigres have gone abroad with all the circulating medium they could lay their hands on, and the Government has much difficulty in maintaining the gold reserve. For my part, I prefer fighting for glory to whistling for money. Fighting is the better profession. You are men. Leave whistling to boys. Follow me into Italy, where there are fertile plains - plains from whose pregnant soil the olive springs at the rate of a million bottles a year, plains through whose lovely lengths there flow rivers of Chianti. Follow me to Italy, where there are opulent towns with clothing-stores on every block, and churches galore, with their poor-boxes bursting with gold. Soldiers, can you resist the alluring prospect?"

"Vive l'Empereur!" cried the army, with one voice.

Napoleon frowned.

"Soldiers!" he cried, "Remember this: you are making history; therefore, pray be accurate. I am not yet Emperor, and you are guilty of an anachronism of a most embarrassing sort. Some men make history in a warm room with pen and ink, aided by guide-books and collections of anecdotes. Leave anachronisms and inaccuracies to them. For ourselves, we must carve it out with our swords and cannon; we must rubricate our pages with our gore, and punctuate our periods with our bayonets. Let it not be said by future ages that we held our responsibilities lightly and were careless of facts, and to that end don't refer to me as Emperor until you are more familiar with dates. When

John Kendrick Bangs

we have finished with Italy I'll take you to the land where dates grow. Meanwhile, restez tranquille, as they say in French, and breathe all the air you want. France can afford you that in unstinted measure."

"Vive Bonaparte!" cried the army, taking the rebuke in good part.

"Now you're shouting," said Napoleon, with a smile. "You're a good army, and if you stick by me you'll wear diamonds."

"We have forgotten one thing," said Barras a few days later, on the eve of Napoleon's departure. "We haven't any casus belli."

"What's that?" said Napoleon, who had been so busy with his preparations that he had forgotten most of his Greek and Latin.

"Cause for war," said Barras. "Where were you educated? If you are going to fight the Italians you've got to have some principle to fight for."

"That's precisely what we are going to fight for," said Napoleon. "We're a bankrupt people. We're going to get some principal to set us up in business. We may be able to float some bonds in Venice."

"True," returned Barras; "but that, after all, is mere highway robbery."

"Well, all I've got to say," retorted Napoleon, with a sneer - "all I've got to say is that if your Directory can't find something in the attitude of Italy towards the Republic to take offence at, the sooner it goes out of business the better. I'll leave that question entirely to you fellows at Paris. I can't do everything. You look after the casus, and I'll take care of the belli."

This plan was adopted. The Directory, after discussing various causes for action, finally decided that an attack on Italy was necessary for three reasons. First, because the alliance between the kings of Sardinia and Austria was a menace to the Republic, and must therefore be broken. Second, the Austrians were too near the Rhine for France's comfort, and must be diverted before they had drunk all the wine of the country, of which the French were very fond; and, third, His Holiness the Pope had taken little interest in the now infidel France, and must therefore be humiliated. These were the reasons for the war settled upon by the government, and as they were as satisfactory to Napoleon as any others, he gave the order which set the army of Italy in motion.

"How shall we go, General?" asked Augereau, one of his subordinates. "Over the Alps?"

"Not this time," returned Napoleon. "It is too cold. The army has no ear-tabs. We'll skirt the Alps, and maybe the skirt will make them warmer."

This the army proceeded at once to do, and within a month the first object of the war was accomplished.

The Sardinian king was crushed, and the army found itself in possession of food, drink, and clothes to a surfeit. Bonaparte's pride at his success was great but not over-weening.

"Soldiers!" he cried, "you have done well. So have I. Hannibal crossed the Alps. We didn't; but we got here just the same. You have provided yourselves with food and clothes, and declared a dividend for the Treasury of France which will enable the Directory to buy itself a new hat through which to address the people. You have reason to be proud of yourselves. Pat yourselves on your backs with my compliments, but remember one thing. Our tickets are to Milan, and no stop-overs are allowed. Therefore, do not as yet relax your efforts. Milan is an imperial city. The guide-books tell us that its cathedral is a beauty, the place is full of pictures, and the opera-house finished in 1779 is the largest in the world. It can be done in two days, and the hotels are good. Can you, therefore, sleep here?"

"No, no!" cried the army.

"Then," cried Napoleon, tightening his reins and lifting his horse on to its hind-legs and holding his sword aloft, "A Milan!"

"How like a statue he looks," said Lannes, admiringly.

"Yes," replied Augereau, "you'd think he was solid brass."

The Austrian troops were now concentrated behind the Po, but Napoleon soon outgeneralled their leaders, drove them back to the Adda, and himself pushed on to the Bridge of Lodi, which connected the east and west branches of that river.

"When I set out for the P. O. P. E.," said Napoleon, "I'm not going to stop halfway and turn back at the P. O. We've got the Austrians over the Adda, and that's just where we want them. I had a dream once about the Bridge of Lodi, and it's coming true now or never. We'll take a few of our long divisions, cross the Adda, and subtract a few fractions of the remainder now left the Austrians. This will destroy their enthusiasm, and Milan will be ours."

The words were prophetic, for on the 10th of May the French did precisely what their commander had said they would do, and on the fourteenth day of May the victorious French entered Milan, the wealthy capital of Lombardy.

"Curious fact," said Napoleon. "In times of peace if a man needs a tonic you give him iron, and it builds him up; but in war if you give the troops iron it bowls 'em down. Look at those Austrians; they've got nervous prostration of the worst sort."

"They got too much iron," said Lannes.

"Too much tonic is worse than none. A man can stand ten or twenty grains of iron, but forty pounds is rather upsetting."

"True," acquiesced Napoleon. "Well, it was a great fight, and I have only one regret. I do wish you'd had a Kodak to take a few snap-shots of me at that Bridge of Lodi. I'd like to send some home to the family. It would have reminded brother Joseph of old times to see me dashing over that bridge, prodding its planks with my heels until it fairly creaked with pain. It would have made a good frontispiece for Bourrienne's book too. And now, my dear Lannes, what shall we do with ourselves for the next five days? Get out your Baedecker and let us see this imperial city of the Lombards."

"There's one matter we must arrange first," said Augereau; "we haven't any stable accommodations to speak of."

"What's the matter with the stalls at the opera-house?" suggested Napoleon. "As I told the troops the other day, it's the biggest theatre in the world. You ought to be able to stable the horses there and lodge the men in the boxes."

"The horses would look well sitting in orchestra chairs, wouldn't they?" said Augereau. "It's not feasible. As for the boxes, they're mostly held by subscribers."

"Then stable them in the picture-galleries," said the general. "It will be good discipline."

"The people will call that sacrilege," returned Augereau.

"Not if we remove the pictures," said Bonaparte. "We'll send the pictures to Paris."

Accordingly this was done, and the galleries of France were thereby much enriched. We mention these details at length, because Napoleon has been severely criticised for thus impoverishing Italy, as well as for his so-called contempt of art - a criticism which, in the face of this accurate version, must fall to the ground. The pictures were sent by him to Paris merely to preserve them, and, as he himself said, a propos of the famous Da Vinci, beneath which horses and men alike were quartered: "I'd have sent that too, but to do it I'd have had to send the whole chapel or scrape the picture off the wall. These Italians should rather thank than condemn me for leaving it where it was. Mine was not an army of destruction, but a Salvation Army of the highest type."

"You made mighty few converts for a Salvation Army," said Talleyrand, to whom this remark was addressed.

"That's where you are wrong," said Napoleon. "I made angels of innumerable Austrians, and converted quite a deal of Italian into French territory."

It was hardly to be doubted that Napoleon's successes would arouse jealousies in Paris, and the Directory, fearing the hold the victorious general was acquiring upon the people, took steps to limit his powers. Bonaparte instantly resigned his command and threatened to return to Paris, which so frightened the government that they refused to accept his resignation.

From this time on for nearly a year Napoleon's career was a succession of victories. He invaded the Papal States, and acquired millions of francs and hundreds of pictures. He chastised all who opposed his sway, and, after pursuing the Austrians as far as Leoben, within sight of Vienna, he humbled the haughty Emperor Joseph.

"I'll recognize your Republic," said the Emperor at last, finding that there was nothing else to be done.

"Thanks," said Napoleon - "I thought you would; but I don't know whether the Republic will recognize you. She doesn't even know you by sight."

"Is that all you want?" asked the Emperor, anxiously.

"For the present, yes. Some day I may come back for something else," returned Napoleon, significantly. "And, by-the-way, when you are sending your card to the French people just enclose a small remittance of a few million francs, not necessarily for publication, but as a guarantee of good faith. Don't send all you've got, but just enough. You may want to marry off one of your daughters some day, and it will be well to save something for her dowry."

It was in little acts of this nature that Napoleon showed his wonderful foresight. One would almost incline to believe from this particular incident that Bonaparte foresaw the Marie-Louise episode in his future career.

The Austrians humbled, Napoleon turned his attention to Venice. Venice had been behaving in a most exasperating fashion, and the conqueror felt that the time had come to take the proud City of the Sea in hand.

"If the Venetians have any brains," said he to Bourrienne, who joined him about this time, secretly representing, it is said, a newspaper-syndicate service, "they'll put on all the sail they've got and take their old city out to sea. They're in for the worst ducking they ever got."

"I'm afraid you'll find them hard to get at," said Bourrienne. "That lagoon is a wet place."

"Oh, as for that," said Bonaparte, "a little water will do the army good. We've been fighting so hard it's been months since they've had a good tubbing, and a swim won't hurt them. Send Lannes here." In a few minutes Lannes entered Bonaparte's tent.

"Lannes, we're off for Venice. Provide the army with over-shoes, and have our luggage checked through," said Bonaparte.

"Yes, General."

"Can Augereau swim?"

"I don't know, General."

"Well, find out, and if he can't we'll get him a balloon."

Thus, taking every precaution for the comfort of his men and the safety of his officers, Napoleon set out. Venice, hearing of his approach, was filled with consternation, and endeavored to temporize. The Doges offered millions if Bonaparte would turn his attention to others, to which Napoleon made this spirited reply: "Venetians, tell the Doges, with my compliments, that I am coming. The wealth of the Indies couldn't change my mind. They offer me stocks and bonds; well, I believe their stocks and bonds to be as badly watered as their haughty city, and I'll have none of them. I'll bring my stocks with me, and your Doges will sit in them. I'll bring my bonds, and your nobles shall put them on and make them clank. You've been drowning Frenchmen every chance you've had. It will now be my pleasing duty to make you do a little gurgling on your own account. You'll find out for the first time in your lives what it is to be in the swim. Put on your bathing-suits and prepare for the avenger. The lions of St. Marc must lick the dust."

"We have no dust, General," said one of the messengers.

"Then you'd better get some," retorted Napoleon, "for you will have to come down with it to the tune of millions."

True to his promise, Napoleon appeared at the lagoon on the 31st of May, and the hitherto haughty Venice fell with a splash that could be heard for miles, first having sent five ships of war, 3,000,000 francs, as many more in naval stores, twenty of her best pictures, the bronze horses of the famous church, five hundred manuscripts, and one apology to the French Republic as the terms of peace. The bronze horses were subsequently returned, but what became of the manuscripts we do not know. They probably would have been returned also - a large portion of them, at least - if postage-stamps had been enclosed. This is mere theory, of course; but it is rendered reasonable by the fact that this is the usual fate of most manuscripts; nor is there any record of their having been published in the Moniteur, the only periodical which the French government was printing at that time.

As for Bonaparte, it was as balm to his soul to humble the haughty Doges, whose attitude towards him had always been characterized by a superciliousness which filled him with resentment.

"It did me good," he said, many years after, with a laugh, "to see those Doges swimming up and down the Grand Canal in their state robes, trying to look dignified, while I stood on the sidewalk and asked them why they didn't come in out of the wet."

CHAPTER VI

MONTEBELLO - PARIS - EGYPT 1797-1799

Josephine now deemed it well to join her lord at Milan. There had been so many only women he had ever loved that she was not satisfied to remain at Paris while he was conducting garden-parties at the Castle of Montebello. Furthermore, Bonaparte himself wished her to be present.

"This Montebello life is, after all, little else than a dress rehearsal for what is to come," he said, confidentially, to Bourrienne, "and Josephine can't afford to be absent. It's a great business, this being a Dictator and having a court of your own, and I'm inclined to think I shall follow it up as my regular profession after I've conquered a little more of the earth."

Surrounded by every luxury, and in receipt for the first time in his life of a steady income, Bonaparte carried things with a high hand. He made treaties with various powers without consulting the Directory, for whom every day he felt a growing contempt.

"What is the use of my consulting the Directory, anyhow?" he asked. "If it were an Elite Directory it might be worth while, but it isn't. I shall, therefore, do as I please, and if they don't like what I do I'll ratify it myself."

Ambassadors waited upon him as though he were a king, and

when one ventured to disagree with the future Emperor he wished he hadn't. Cobentzel, the envoy of the Austrian ruler, soon discovered this.

"I refuse to accept your ultimatum," said he one day to Napoleon, after a protracted conference.

"You do, eh?" - said Napoleon, picking up a vase of delicate workmanship. "Do you see this jug?"

"Yes," said Cobentzel.

"Well," continued Napoleon, dropping it to the floor, where it was shattered into a thousand pieces, "do you see it now?"

"I do," said Cobentzel; "what then?"

"It has a mate," said Napoleon, significantly; "and if you do not accept my ultimatum I'll smash the other one upon your plain but honest countenance."

Cobentzel accepted the ultimatum.

Bonaparte's contempt for the Directory was beginning to be shared by a great many of the French, and, to save themselves, the "Five Sires of the Luxembourg," as the Directory were called, resolved on a brilliant stroke, which involved no less a venture than the invasion of England. Bonaparte, hearing of this, and anxious to see London, of which he had heard much, left Italy and returned to Paris.

"If there's a free tour of England to be had, Josephine," said he, "I am the man to have it. Besides, this climate of Italy is getting pretty hot for an honest man. I've refused twenty million francs in bribes in two weeks. If they'd offered another sou I'm afraid I'd have taken it. I will therefore go to Paris, secure the command of the army of England, and pay a few of my respects to George Third, Esq. I hear a great many English drop their h's; I'll see if I can't make 'em drop their l. s. d.'s

John Kendrick Bangs

as well."

Arrived in Paris, Bonaparte was much courted by everybody.

"I have arrived," he said, with a grim smile. "Even my creditors are glad to see me, and I'll show them that I have not forgotten them by running up a few more bills."

This he did, going to the same tradesmen that he had patronized in his days of poverty. To his hatter, whom he owed for his last five hats, he said:

"They call me haughty here; they say I am cold. Well, I am cold. I've shivered on the Alps several times since I was here last, and it has chilled my nature. It has given me the grip, so to speak, and when I lose my grip the weather will be even colder. Give me a hat, my friend."

"What size?" asked the hatter.

"The same," said Bonaparte, with a frown. "Why do you ask?"

"I was told your head had swelled," returned the hatter, meekly.

"They shall pay for this," murmured Napoleon, angrily.

"I am glad," said the hatter, with a sigh. "I was wondering who'd pay for it."

"Oh, you were, eh?" said Napoleon. "Well, wonder no more. Get out your books."

The hatter did so.

"Now charge it," said Napoleon.

"To whom?" asked the hatter.

"Those eminent financiers, Profit & Loss," said Napoleon, with a laugh, as he left the shop. "That's what I call a most successful hat-talk," he added, as he told Bourrienne of the incident later in the day.

"How jealous they all are!" said Bourrienne. "The idea of your having a swelled head is ridiculous."

"Of course," said Napoleon; "all I've got is a proper realization of 'Whom I Am,' as they say in Boston. But wait, my boy, wait. When I put a crown on my head -"

What Bonaparte would have said will never be known, for at that moment the general's servant announced Mme. Sans Gene, his former laundress, and that celebrated woman, unconventional as ever, stalked into the room. Napoleon looked at her coldly.

"You are -?" he queried.

"Your former laundress," she replied.

"Ah, and you want -?"

"My pay," she retorted.

"I am sorry, madame," said the General, "but the expenses of my Italian tour have been very great, and I am penniless. I will, however, assist you to the full extent of my power. Here are three collars and a dress-shirt. If you will launder them I will wear them to the state ball to-morrow evening, and will tell all my rich and influential friends who did them up, and if you wish I will send you a letter saying that I patronized your laundry once two years ago, and have since used no other."

These anecdotes, unimportant in themselves, are valuable in that they refute the charges made against General Bonaparte at this time - first, that he returned from Egypt with a fortune, and, second, that he carried himself with a hauteur which rendered him unapproachable.

For various reasons the projected invasion of England was abandoned, and the expedition to Egypt was substituted. This pleased Napoleon equally as well.

"I wasn't stuck on the English invasion, anyhow," he said, in writing to Joseph. "In the first place, they wanted me to go in October, when the London season doesn't commence until spring, and, in the second place, I hate fogs and mutton-chops. Egypt is more to my taste. England would enervate me. Egypt, with the Desert of Sahara in its backyard, will give me plenty of sand, and if you knew what projects I have in mind - which, of course, you don't, for you never knew anything, my dear Joseph - you'd see how much of that I need."

The Directory were quite as glad to have Napoleon go to Egypt as he was to be sent. Their jealousy of him was becoming more painful to witness every day.

"If he goes to England," said Barras, "he'll conquer it, sure as fate; and it will be near enough for excursion steamers to take the French people over to see him do it. If that happens we are lost."

"He'll conquer Egypt, though, and he'll tell about it in such a way that he will appear twice as great," suggested Carnot. "Seems to me we'd better sell out at once and be done with it."

"Not so," said Moulin. "Let him go to Egypt. Very likely he'll fall off a pyramid there and break his neck."

"Or get sunstruck," suggested Barras.

"There's no question about it in my mind," said Gohier. "Egypt is the place. If he escapes the pyramids or sunstroke, there are still the lions and the simoon, not to mention the rapid tides of the Red Sea. Why, he just simply can't get back alive. I vote for Egypt."

Thus it happened that on the 19th day of May, 1798, with an army of forty thousand men and a magnificent staff of picked officers, Napoleon embarked for Egypt.

"I'm glad we're off," said he to the sailor who had charge of his steamer-chair. "I've got to hurry up and gain some more victories or these French will forget me. A man has to make a three-ringed circus of himself to keep his name before the public these days."

"What are you fightin' for this time, sir?" asked the sailor, who had not heard that war had been declared - "ile paintin's or pyramids?"

"I am going to free the people of the East from the oppressor," said Napoleon, loftily.

"And it's a noble work, your honor," said the sailor. "Who is it that's oppressin' these people down East?"

"You'll have to consult the Directory," said Napoleon, coldly. "Leave me; I have other things to think of."

On the 10th of June Malta was reached, and the Knights of St. John, long disused to labor of any sort, like many other knights of more modern sort, surrendered in most hospitable fashion, inviting Napoleon to come ashore and accept the freedom of the island or anything else he might happen to want. His reply was characteristic:

"Tell the Knights of Malta to attend to their cats. I'm after continents, not islands," said he; and with this, leaving a detachment of troops to guard his new acquisition, he proceeded to Alexandria, which he reached on the 1st of July. Here, in the midst of a terrible storm and surf, Napoleon landed his forces, and immediately made a proclamation to the people.

"Fellahs!" he cried, "I have come. The newspapers say to

destroy your religion. As usual, they prevaricate. I have come to free you. All you who have yokes to shed prepare to shed them now. I come with the olive-branch in my hand. Greet me with outstretched palms. Do not fight me for I am come to save you, and I shall utterly obliterate any man, be he fellah, Moujik, or even the great Marmalade himself, who prefers fighting to being saved. We may not look it, but we are true Mussulmen. If you doubt it, feel our muscle. We have it to burn. Desert the Mamelukes and be saved. The Pappylukes are here."

On reading this proclamation Alexandria immediately fell, and Bonaparte, using the Koran as a guide-book, proceeded on his way up the Nile. The army suffered greatly from the glare and burning of the sun-scorched sand, and from the myriads of pestiferous insects that infested the country; but Napoleon cheered them on. "Soldiers!" he cried, when they complained, "if this were a summer resort, and you were paying five dollars a day for a room at a bad hotel, you'd think yourselves in luck, and you'd recommend your friends to come here for a rest. Why not imagine this to be the case now? Brace up. We'll soon reach the pyramids, and it's a mighty poor pyramid that hasn't a shady side. On to Cairo!"

"It's easy enough for you to talk," murmured one. "You've got a camel to ride on and we have to walk."

"Well, Heaven knows," retorted Napoleon, pointing to his camel, "camel riding isn't like falling off a log. At first I was carried away with it, but for the last two days it has made me so sea-sick I can hardly see that hump."

After this there was no more murmuring, but Bonaparte did not for an instant relax his good-humor.

"The water is vile," said Dessaix, one morning.

"Why not drink milk, then?" asked the commander.

"Milk! I'd love to," returned Dessaix; "but where shall I find milk?"

"At the dairy," said Napoleon, with a twinkle in his eye.

"What dairy?" asked Dessaix, not observing the twinkle.

"The dromedary," said Napoleon, with a roar.

Little incidents like this served to keep the army in good spirits until the 21st of July, when they came in sight of the pyramids. Instantly Napoleon called a halt, and the army rested. The next day, drawing them up in line, the General addressed them. "Soldiers!" he cried, pointing to the pyramids, "from the summits of those pyramids forty centuries look down upon you. You can't see them, but they are there. No one should look down upon the French, not even a century. Therefore, I ask you, shall we allow the forces of the Bey, his fellahs and his Tommylukes, to drive us into the desert of Sahara, bag and baggage, to subsist on a sea-less seashore for the balance of our days, particularly when they haven't any wheels on their cannon?"

"No, no!" cried the army.

"Then up sail and away!" cried Bonaparte. "This is to be no naval affair, but the army of the Bey awaits us."

"Tell the band to play a Wagner march," he whispered, hastily, to his aide-de-camp. "It'll make the army mad, and what we need now is wrath."

So began the battle of the Pyramids. The result is too well known to readers of contemporary history to need detailed statement here. All day long it raged, and when night fell Cairo came with it. Napoleon, worn out with fatigue, threw himself down on a pyramid to rest.

"Ah!" he said, as he breathed a sigh of relief, "what a glorious day! We've beat 'em! Won't the Directory be glad? M. Barras will be more M. Barrassed than ever." Then, turning and tapping on the door of the massive pile, he whispered, softly: "Ah! Ptolemy, my man, it's a pity you've no windows in this tomb. You'd have seen a pretty sight this day. Kleber," he added, turning to that general, "do you know why Ptolemy inside this pyramid and I outside of it are alike?"

"I cannot guess, General," said Kleber. "Why?"

"We're both 'in it'!" returned Napoleon, retiring to his tent.

Later on in the evening, summoning Bourrienne, the victor said to him:

"Mr. Secretary, I have a new autograph. If Ptolemy can spell his name with a 'p,' why shouldn't I? I'm not going to have history say that a dead mummy could do things I couldn't. Pnapoleon would look well on a state paper."

"No doubt," said Bourrienne; "but every one now says that you copy Caesar. Why give them the chance to call you an imitator of Ptolemy also?"

"True, my friend, true," returned Napoleon, in a tone of disappointment. "I had not thought of that. When you write my autographs for the children of these Jennylukes -"

"Mamelukes, General," corrected Bourrienne.

"Ah, yes - I always get mixed in these matters - for the children of these Mamelukes, you may stick to the old form. Goodnight."

And with that the conqueror went to sleep as peacefully as a little child.

Had Bonaparte now returned to France he would have saved himself much misery. King of fire though he had become in the eyes of the vanquished, his bed was far from being one of roses.

"In a climate like that," he observed, sadly, many years after, "I'd rather have been an ice baron. Africa got entirely too hot to cut any ice with me. Ten days after I had made my friend Ptolemy turn over in his grave, Admiral Nelson came along with an English fleet and challenged our Admiral Brueys to a shooting-match for the championship of Aboukir Bay. Brueys, having heard of what magazine writers call the ships of the desert in my control, supposing them to be frigates and not camels, imagined himself living in Easy Street, and accepted the challenge. He expected me to sail around to the other side of Nelson, and so have him between two fires. Well, I don't go to sea on camels, as you know, and the result was that after a twenty-four-hour match the camels were the only ships we had left. Nelson had won the championship, laid the corner-stone of monuments to himself all over English territory, cut me off from France, and added three thousand sea-lubbers to my force, for that number of French sailors managed to swim ashore during the fight. I manned the camels with them immediately, but it took them months to get their land legs on, and the amount of grog they demanded would have made a quick-sand of the Desert of Sahara, all of which was embarrassing."

But Napoleon did not show his embarrassment to those about him. He took upon himself the government of Egypt, opened canals, and undertook to behave like a peaceable citizen for a while.

"I needed rest, and I got it," he said. "Sitting on the apex of the pyramids, I could see the whole world at my feet, and whatever others may say to the contrary, it was there that I began to get a clear view of my future. It seemed to me that from that lofty altitude, chumming, as I was, with the forty centuries I have already alluded to, I could see two ways at once, that every glance could penetrate eternity; but I realize now that what I really got was only a bird's-eye view of the future. I didn't see that speck of a St. Helena. If I had, in the height of my power I should have despatched an expedition of sappers and miners to blow it up."

Quiescence might as well be expected of a volcano, however, as from a man of Bonaparte's temperament, and it was not long before he was again engaged in warfare, but not with his old success; and finally, the plague having attacked his army, Bonaparte, too tender-hearted to see it suffer, leaving opium for the sick and instructions for Kleber, whom he appointed his successor, set sail for France once more in September, 1799.

"Remember, Kleber, my boy," he said, in parting, "these Mussulmen are a queer lot. Be careful how you treat them. If you behave like a Christian you're lost. I don't want to go back to France, but I must. I got a view of the next three years from the top of Cheops last night just before sunset, and if that view is to be carried out my presence in Paris is positively required. The people are tired of the addresses given by the old Directory, and they're seriously thinking of getting out a new one, and I want to be on hand either to edit it or to secure my appointment to some lucrative consulship."

"You! - a man of your genius after a consulship?" queried Kleber, astonished.

"Yes, I have joined the office-seekers, General; but wait till you hear what consulship it is. The American consul-generalship at London is worth $70,000 a year, but mine - mine in contrast to that is as golf to muggins."

"And what shall I tell the reporters about that Jaffa business if they come here? That poison scandal is sure to come up," queried Kleber.

"Treat them well. Tell the truth if you know it, and - ah - invite them to dinner," said Bonaparte. "Give them all the delicacies of the season. When you serve the poisson, let it be with one 's,' and, to make assurance doubly sure, flavor the wines with the quickest you have."

"Quickest what?" asked Kleber, who was slightly obtuse.

"Humph!" sneered Napoleon. "On second thoughts, if reporters bother you, take them swimming where the crocodiles are thickest - only either don't bathe with them yourself, or wear your mail bathing-suit. Furthermore, remember that what little of the army is left are my children."

"What?" cried the obtuse Kleber. "All those?"

"They are my children, Kleber," said Napoleon, his voice shaking with emotion. "I am young to be the head of so large a family, but the fact remains as I have said. They may feel badly at my going away and leaving them even with so pleasing a hired man as yourself, but comfort them, let them play in the sand all they please, and if they want to know why papa has gone away, tell them I've gone to Paris to buy them some candy."

With these words Napoleon embarked, and on the 16th of October Paris received him with open arms. That night the members of the Directory came down with chills and fever.

CHAPTER VII

THE 19TH BRUMAIRE - CONSUL -
THE TUILERIES - CAROLINE 1799

"There is no question about my greatness now," said Napoleon, as he meditated upon his position. "Even if the Directory were not jealous and the people enthusiastic, the number of relatives I have discovered in the last ten days would show that things are going my way. I have had congratulatory messages from 800 aunts, 950 uncles, and about 3800 needy cousins since my arrival. It is queer how big a family a lonely man finds he has when his star begins to twinkle. Even Joseph is glad see me now, and I am told that the ice-cream men serve little vanilla Napoleons at all the swell dinners. Bourrienne, our time has come! Get out my most threadbare uniform, fray a few of my collars at the edges, and shoot a few holes in my hat. I'll go out and take a walk along the Avenue de l'Opera, where the people can see me."

"There isn't any such street in Paris yet, General," said Bourrienne, getting out his Paris guide-book.

"Well, there ought to be," said Napoleon.

"What streets are there? I must be seen or I'll be forgotten."

"What's the matter with a lounge in front of the Luxembourg? That will make a contrast that can't help affect the populace. You, the conqueror, ill-clad, unshaven, and with a hat full of bullet-holes, walking outside the palace, with the incompetent Directors lodged comfortably inside, will make a scene that is bound to give the people food for thought."

"Well said!" cried Bonaparte. "Here are the pistols go out into the woods and prepare the hat. I'll fray the collars."

This was done, and the effect was instantaneous. The public perceived the point, and sympathy ran so high that a public dinner was offered to the returned warrior.

"I have no use for pomp, Mr. Toast-master," he said, as he rose to speak at this banquet. "I am not a good after-dinner speaker, but I want the people of France to know that I am grateful for this meal. I rise only to express the thanks of a hungry man for this timely contribution to his inner self, and I wish to add that I should not willingly have added to the already heavy tax upon the pockets of a patriotic people by accepting this dinner, if it were not for the demands of nature. It is only the direst necessity that brings me here; for one must eat, and I cannot beg."

These remarks, as may well be imagined, sent a thrill of enthusiasm throughout France and filled the Directory with consternation. The only cloud upon Bonaparte's horizon was a slight coldness which arose between himself and Josephine. She had gone to meet him on his arrival at Frejus, but by some odd mistake took the road to Burgundy, while Napoleon came by way of Lyons. They therefore missed each other.

"I could not help it," she said, when Napoleon jealously chided her. "I've travelled very little, and the geography of France always did puzzle me."

"It is common sense that should have guided you, not knowledge of geography. When I sail into Port, you sail into Burgundy - you, the only woman I ever loved!" cried Napoleon, passionately. "Hereafter, madame, for the sake of our step-children, be more circumspect. At this time I cannot afford a trip to South Dakota for the purpose of a quiet divorce, nor would a public one pay at this juncture; but I give you fair warning that I shall not forget this escapade, and once we are settled in the - the Whatistobe, I shall remember, and another only woman I have ever loved will dawn upon your horizon."

Bonaparte was now besieged by all the military personages of France. His home became the Mecca of soldiers of all kinds, and in order to hold their interest the hero of the day found it necessary to draw somewhat upon the possessions which the people were convinced he was without. Never an admirer of consistency, France admired this more than ever. It was a paradox that this poverty-stricken soldier should entertain so lavishly, and the people admired the nerve which prompted him to do it, supposing, many of them, that his creditors were men of a speculative nature, who saw in the man a good-paying future investment.

Thus matters went until the evening of the 17th Brumaire, when Napoleon deemed that he had been on parade long enough, and that the hour demanded action.

"This is the month of Bromide," he said.

"Brumaire," whispered Bourrienne.

"I said Bromide," retorted Napoleon, "and the people are asleep. Bromide has that effect. That is why I call it Bromide, and I have as much right to name my months as any one else. Wherefore I repeat, this is the month of Bromide, and the people are asleep! I will now wake them up. The garrisons of Paris and the National Guard have asked me to review them, and I'm going to do it, and I've a new set of tictacs."

"Tactics, General, tactics," implored Bourrienne.

"There is no use discussing words, Mr. Secretary," retorted

Bonaparte. "It has always been the criticism of my opponents that I didn't know a tactic from a bedtick - well, perhaps I don't; and for that reason I am not going to talk about tactics with which I am not familiar, but I shall speak of tictacs, which is a game I have played from infancy, and of which I am a master. I'm going to get up a new government, Bourrienne. Summon all the generals in town, including Bernadotte. They're all with me except Bernadotte, and he'll be so unpleasant about what I tell him to do that he'll make all the others so mad they'll stick by me through thick and thin. If there's any irritating work to be done, let Joseph do it. He has been well trained in the art of irritation. I have seen Sieyes and Ducos, and have promised them front seats in the new government which my tictacs are to bring about. Barras won't have the nerve to oppose me, and Gohier and Moulin have had the ague for weeks. We'll have the review, and my first order to the troops will be to carry humps; the second will be to forward march; and the third will involve the closing of a long lease, in my name, of the Luxembourg Palace, with a salary connected with every room in the house."

It is needless for us to go into details. The review came off as Napoleon wished, and his orders were implicitly obeyed, with the result that on the 19th of Brumaire the Directory was filed away, and Napoleon Bonaparte, with Sieyes and Ducos as fellow-consuls, were called upon to save France from anarchy.

"Well, Josephine," said Bonaparte, on the evening of the 19th, as he put his boots outside of the door of his new apartment in the Luxembourg, "this is better than living in a flat, and I must confess I find the feather-beds of the palace more inviting than a couch of sand under a date-tree in Africa."

"And what are you going to do next?" asked Josephine.

"Ha!" laughed Napoleon, blowing out the candle. "There's a woman's curiosity for you! The continuation of this entertaining story, my love, will be found in volume two of Bourrienne's attractive history, From the Tow-path to the

Tuileries, now in course of preparation, and for sale by all accredited agents at the low price of ten francs a copy."

With this remark Napoleon jumped into bed, and on the authority of M. le Comte de Q-, at this time Charge a Affaires of the Luxembourg, and later on Janitor of the Tuileries, was soon dreaming of the Empire.

The Directory overthrown, Bonaparte turned his attention to the overthrow of the Consulate.

"Gentlemen," he said to his fellow-consuls, "I admire you personally very much, and no doubt you will both of you agree in most matters, but as I am fearful lest you should disagree on matters of importance, and so break that beautiful friendship which I am pleased to see that you have for each other, I shall myself cast a deciding vote in all matters, large or small. This will enable you to avoid differences, and to continue in that spirit of amity which I have always so much admired in your relations. You can work as hard as you please, but before committing yourselves to anything, consult me, not each other. What is a Consul for if not for a consultation?"

Against this Sieyes and Ducos were inclined to rebel, but Bonaparte soon dispelled their opposition. Ringing his bell, he summoned an aide-de-camp, whispered a few words in his ear, and then leaned quietly back in his chair. The aide-de-camp retired, and two minutes later the army stationed without began shouting most enthusiastically for Bonaparte. The General walked to the window and bowed, and the air was rent with huzzas and vivas.

"I guess he's right," whispered Sieyes, as the shouting grew more and more vigorous.

"Guess again," growled Ducos.

"You were saying, gentlemen - ?" said Bonaparte, returning.

"That we are likely to have rain before long," said Sieyes, quickly.

"I shouldn't be surprised," returned Napoleon, "and I'd advise you laymen to provide yourselves with umbrellas when the rain begins. I, as a soldier, shall not feel the inclemency of the weather that is about to set in. And, by-the-way, Sieyes, please prepare a new Constitution for France, providing for a single-headed commission to rule the country. Ducos, you need rest. Pray take a vacation until further notice; I'll attend to matters here. On your way down-stairs knock at Bourrienne's door, and tell him I want to see him. I have a few more memoirs for his book."

With these words Bonaparte adjourned the meeting. Sieyes went home and drew up the Constitution, and M. Ducos retired to private life for rest. The Constitution of Sieyes was a clever instrument, but Bonaparte rendered it unavailing. It provided for three consuls, but one of them was practically given all the power, and the others became merely his clerks.

"This is as it should be," said Bonaparte, when by 4,000,000 votes the Constitution was ratified by the people. "These three-headed governments are apt to be failures, particularly when two of the heads are worthless. Cambaceres makes a first-rate bottle-holder, and Lebrun is a competent stenographer, but as for directing France in the line of her destiny they are of no use. I will now move into the Tuileries. I hate pomp, as I have often said, but Paris must be dazzled. We can't rent the palace for a hotel, and it's a pity to let so much space go to waste. Josephine, pack up your trunk, and tell Bourrienne to have a truckman here at eleven sharp. To-morrow night we will dine at the Tuileries, and for Heaven's sake see to it that the bottles are cold and the birds are hot. For the sake of the Republic also, that we may not appear too ostentatious in our living, you may serve cream with the demi-tasse."

Once established in the Tuileries, Bonaparte became in reality

the king, and his family who had for a long time gone a-
begging began to assume airs of importance, which were
impressive. His sisters began to be invited out, and were
referred to by the society papers as most eligible young
persons. Their manner, however, was somewhat in advance of
their position. Had their brother been actually king and
themselves of royal birth they could not have conducted themselves more haughtily. This was never so fully demonstrated as
when, at a ball given in their honor at Marseilles, an old friend
of the family who had been outrageously snubbed by Caroline,
asked her why she wore her nose turned up so high.

"Because my brother is reigning in Paris," she retorted.

In this she but voiced the popular sentiment, and the remark
was received with applause; and later, Murat, who had
distinguished himself as a military man, desirous of allying
himself with the rising house, demanded her hand in marriage.

"You?" cried the First Consul. "Why, Murat, your father kept
an inn."

"I know it," said Murat. "But what of that?"

"My blood must not be mixed with yours, that's what," said
Bonaparte.

"Very well, Mr. Bonaparte," said Murat, angrily, "let it be so;
but I tell you one thing: When you see the bills Caroline is
running up you'll find it would have been money in your
pocket to transfer her to me. As for the inn business, my
governor never served such atrocious meals at his table-d'hote
as you serve to your guests at state banquets, and don't you
forget it."

Whether these arguments overcame Bonaparte's scruples or
not is not known, but a few days later he relented, and
Caroline became the wife of Murat.

"I never regretted it," said Bonaparte, some years later. "Murat was a good brother-in-law to me, and he taught me an invaluable lesson in the giving of state banquets, which was that one portion is always enough for three. And as for parting with my dear sister, that did not disturb me very much; for, truly, Talleyrand, Caroline was the only woman I never loved."

CHAPTER VIII

THE ALPS - THE EMPIRE -
THE CORONATION 1800-1804

"Observe," said Bonaparte, now that he was seated on the consular throne, "that one of my biographers states that, under a man of ordinary vigor this new Constitution of Sieyes and another our government would be free and popular, but that under myself it has become an unlimited monarchy. That man is right. I am now a potentate of the most potent kind. I got a letter from the Bourbons last night requesting me to restore them to the throne. Two years ago they wouldn't have given me their autographs for my collection, but now they want me to get up from my seat in this car of state and let them sit down."

"And you replied - ?" asked Josephine.

"That I didn't care for Bourbon - rye suits me better," laughed the Consul, "unless I can get Scotch, which I prefer at all times. Feeling this way, I cannot permit Louis to come back yet awhile. Meantime, in the hope of replenishing our cellars with a few bottles of Glenlivet, I will write a letter of pacification to George III., one of the most gorgeous rex in Madame Tussaud's collection of living potentates."

This Bonaparte did, asking the English king if he hadn't had enough war for the present. George, through the eyes of his ministers, perceived Bonaparte's point, and replied that he was very desirous for peace himself, but that at present the market seemed to be cornered, and that therefore the war must go on. This reply amused Napoleon.

"It suits me to the ground," he said, addressing Talleyrand. "A year of peace would interfere materially with my future. If Paris were Philadelphia, it would be another thing. There one may rest – there is no popular demand for excitement - Penn was mightier than the sword - but here one has to be in a broil constantly; to be a chef one must be eternally cooking, and the results must be of the kind that requires extra editions of the evening papers. The day the newsboys stop shouting my name, my sun will set for the last time. Even now the populace are murmuring, for nothing startling has occurred this week, which reminds me, I wish to see Fouche. Send him here."

Talleyrand sent for the Minister of Police, who responded to the summons.

"Fouche," said Bonaparte, sternly, "what are we here for, salary or glory?"

"Glory, General."

"Precisely. Now, as head of the Police Department, are you aware that no attempt to assassinate me has been made for two weeks?"

"Yes, General, but -"

"Has the assassin appropriation run out? Have the assassins struck for higher wages, or are you simply careless?" demanded the First Consul. "I warn you, sir, that I wish no excuses, and I will add that unless an attempt is made on my life before ten o'clock to-night, you lose your place. The French people must be kept interested in this performance, and how the deuce it is to be done without advertising I don't know. Go, and remember that I shall be at home to assassins on Thursdays of alternate weeks until further notice."

John Kendrick Bangs

"Your Consulship's wishes shall be respected," said Fouche, with a low bow. "But I must say one word in my own behalf. You were to have had a dynamite bomb thrown at you yesterday by one of my employes, but the brave fellow who was to have stood between you and death disappointed me. He failed to turn up at the appointed hour, and so, of course, the assault didn't come off."

"Couldn't you find a substitute?" demanded Bonaparte.

"I could not," said Fouche. "There aren't many persons in Paris who care for that kind of employment. They'd rather shovel snow."

"You are a gay stage-manager, you are!" snapped Bonaparte. "My brother Joseph is in town, and yet you say you couldn't find a man to be hit by a bomb. Leave me, Fouche. You give me the ennuis."

Fouche departed with Talleyrand, to whom he expressed his indignation at the First Consul's reprimand.

"He insists upon an attempted assassination every week," he said; "and I tell you, Talleyrand, it isn't easy to get these things up. The market is long on real assassins, fellows who'd kill him for the mere fun of hearing his last words, but when it comes to playing to the galleries with a mock attempt with real consequences to the would-be murderers, they fight shy of it."

Nevertheless, Fouche learned from the interview with Bonaparte that the First Consul was not to be trifled with, and hardly a day passed without some exciting episode in this line, in which, of course, Napoleon always came out unscathed and much endeared to the populace. This, however, could not go on forever. The fickle French soon wearied of the series of unsuccessful attempts on the Consul's life, and some began to suspect the true state of affairs.

"They're on to our scheme, General," said Fouche, after a

while. "You've got to do something new."

"What would you suggest?" asked Napoleon, wearily.

"Can't you write a book of poems, or a three-volume novel?" suggested Talleyrand.

"Or resign, and let Sieyes run things for a while?" said Fouche. "If they had another Consul for a few months, they'd appreciate what a vaudeville show they lost in you."

"I'd rather cross the Alps," said Bonaparte. "I don't like to resign. Moving is such a nuisance, and I must say I find the Tuileries a very pleasant place of abode. It's more fun than you can imagine rummaging through the late king's old bureau-drawers. Suppose I get up a new army and lead it over the Alps."

"Just the thing," said Talleyrand. "Only it will be a very snowy trip."

"I'm used to snow-balls," said Napoleon, his mind reverting to the episode which brought his career at Brienne to a close. "Just order an army and a mule and I'll set out. Meanwhile, Fouche, see that the Bourbons have a conspiracy to be unearthed in time for the Sunday newspapers every week during my absence. I think it would be well, too, to keep a war-correspondent at work in your office night and day, writing despatches about my progress. Give him a good book on Hannibal's trip to study, and let him fill in a column or two every day with anecdotes about myself, and at convenient intervals unsuccessful attempts to assassinate Josephine may come in handy. Let it be rumored often that I have been overwhelmed by an avalanche - in short, keep the interest up."

So it was that Bonaparte set out upon his perilous expedition over the Great St. Bernard. On the 15th day of May, 1800, the task of starting the army in motion was begun, and on the 18th every column was in full swing. Lannes, with an advance guard armed with snow-shovels, took the lead, and Bonaparte, commanding the rear guard of 35,000 men and the artillery, followed.

"Soldiers!" he cried, as they came near to the snow-bound heights, "we cannot have our plum-cake without its frosting. Like children, we will have the frosting first and the cake later. Lannes and his followers have not cleaned the snow off as thoroughly as I had hoped, but I fancy he has done the best he can, and it is not for us to complain. Let us on. The up-trip will be cold and tedious, but once on the summit of yonder icy ridge we can seat ourselves comfortably on our guns and slide down into the lovely valleys on the other side like a band of merry school-boys on toboggans. Above all, do not forget the chief duty of a soldier in times of peril. In spite of the snow and the ice, in spite of the blizzard and the sleet, keep cool; and, furthermore, remember that in this climate, if your ears don't hurt, it's a sign they are freezing. En avant! Nous sommes le peuple."

The army readily responded to such hopeful words, and as Bonaparte manifested quite as much willingness to walk as the meanest soldier, disdaining to ride, except occasionally, and even then on the back of a mule, he became their idol.

"He does not spare himself any more than he does us," said one of his soldiers, "and he can pack a snow-ball with the best of us."

The General catered, too, to the amusement of his troops, and the brasses of the band broke the icy stillness of the great hills continually.

"Music's the thing," he cried, many years later, "and when we got to the top we had the most original roof-garden you ever saw. It was most inspiring, and the only thing that worried me at all was as to how Fouche was conducting our anecdote and assassination enterprise at home. Once on top of the Alps, the descent was easy. We simply lay down on our arms and slid.

Down the mountain-side we thundered, and the Austrians, when they observed our impetus, gave way before us, and the first thing I knew I skated slam-bang into the Empire. Our avalanchian descent subjugated Italy; frightened the Englishmen to Alexandria, where, in the absence of a well-organized force, they managed to triumph; scared the Pope so thoroughly that he was willing to sign anything I wished; and, best of all, after a few petty delays, convinced the French people that I was too big a man for a mere consulship. It was my chamois-like agility in getting down the Alps that really made me Emperor. As for the army, it fought nobly. It was so thoroughly chilled by the Alpine venture that it fought desperately to get warm. My grenadiers, congealed to their very souls, went where the fire was hottest. They seized bomb-shells while they were yet in the air, warmed their hands upon them, and then threw them back into the enemy's camp, where they exploded with great carnage. They did not even know when they were killed, so benumbed by the cold had they become. In short, those days on the Alps made us invincible. No wonder, then, that in 1804, when I got permanently back to Paris, I found the people ready for an emperor! They were bloody years, those from 1800 to 1804, but it was not entirely my fault. I shed very little myself, but the English and the Austrians and the royalist followers would have it so, and I had to accommodate them. I did not wish to execute the Duc d'Enghien, but he would interfere with Fouche by getting up conspiracies on his own account, when I had given the conspiracy contract to one of my own ministers. The poor fellow had to die. It was a case of no die, no Empire, and I thought it best for the French people that they should have an Empire."

Those who criticise Bonaparte's acts in these years should consider these words, and remember that the great warrior in no case did any of the killing himself.

It was on the 18th of May, 1804, that the Empire was proclaimed and Napoleon assumed his new title amid great rejoicing.

"Now for the coronation," he said. "This thing must go off in style, Fouche. Whom shall I have to crown me?"

"Well," said Fouche, "if you are after a sensation, I'd send for Louis de Bourbon; if you want it to go off easily, I'd send for your old hatter in the Rue de Victoire; if you want to give it a ceremonial touch, I'd send for the Pope, but, on the whole, I rather think I'd do it myself. You picked it up yourself, why not put it on your own head?"

"Good idea," returned Bonaparte. "And highly original. You may increase your salary a hundred francs a week, Fouche. I'll crown myself, but I think it ought to come as a surprise, don't you?"

"Yes," said Fouche. "That is, if you can surprise the French people - which I doubt. If you walked into Notre Dame tomorrow on your hands, with the crown of France on one foot and the diadem of Italy on the other, the people wouldn't be a bit surprised - you're always doing such things."

"Nevertheless," said Napoleon, "we'll surprise them. Send word to the Pope that I want to see him officially on December 2d at Notre Dame. If he hesitates about coming, tell him I'll walk over and bring him myself the first clear day we have."

This plan was followed out to the letter, and the Pope, leaving Rome on the 5th of November, entered Paris to crown the Emperor and Empress of the French on December 2, 1804, as requested. What subsequently followed the world knows. Just as the Pope was about to place the imperial diadem on the brow of Bonaparte, the Emperor seized it and with his own hands placed it there.

"Excuse me, your Holiness," he said, as he did so, "but the joke is on you. This is my crown, and I think I'm a big enough man to hang it up where it belongs."

Pius VII. was much chagrined, but, like the good man that he was, he did not show it, nor did he resent the Emperor's second interference when it came to the crowning of Josephine. The coronation over, Napoleon and Josephine turned to the splendid audience, and marched down the centre aisle to the door, where they entered a superb golden carriage in which, amid the plaudits of the people, they drove to the Tuileries.

"Ah - at last!" said Bonaparte, as he entered the Palace. "I have got there. The thing to do now is to stay there. Ah, me!" he added, with a sigh. "These French - these French! they are as fickle as the only woman I have ever loved. By-the-way, Josephine, what was it you asked me on the way down the aisle? The people howled so I couldn't hear you."

"I only asked you if" - here the Empress hesitated.

"Well? If what?" frowned the Emperor.

"If my crown was on straight," returned Josephine.

"Madame," said the Emperor, sternly, "when you are prompted to ask that question again, remember who gave you that crown, and when you remember that it was I, remember also that when I give anything to anybody I give it to them straight."

Here the Emperor's frown relaxed, and he burst out into laughter.

"But that was a bad break of the organist!" he said.

"Which was that?" asked Josephine.

"Why - didn't you notice when the Pope came in he played 'Tiara Boom-de-ay'?" said Bonaparte, with a roar. "It was awful - I shall have to send him a pourboire."

CHAPTER IX

THE RISE OF THE EMPIRE 1805-1810

"What next?" asked Fouche, the morning after the coronation, as he entered the Emperor's cabinet.

"Breakfast," returned Bonaparte, laconically; "what did you suppose? You didn't think I was going swimming in the Seine, did you?"

"I never think," retorted Fouche.

"That's evident," said Napoleon. "Is the arch-treasurer of my empire up yet? The Empress is going shopping, and wants an appropriation."

"He is, Your Majesty," said Fouche, looking at his memorandum-book. "He rose at 7:30, dressed as usual, parted his hair on the left-hand side, and breakfasted at eight. At 8:15 he read the Moniteur, and sneezed twice while perusing the second column of the fourth page -"

"What is the meaning of these petty details?" cried the Emperor, impatiently.

"I merely wished to show Your Majesty that as the Sherlock Holmes of this administration I am doing my duty. There isn't a man in France who is not being shadowed in your behalf," returned the minister of police.

The Emperor looked out of the window; then, turning to Fouche, he said, the stern, impatient look fading into softness, "Pardon my irritability, Fouche. You are a genius, and I appreciate you, though I may not always show it. I didn't sleep well last night, and in consequence I am not unduly amiable this morning."

"Your Majesty is not ill, I trust?" said Fouche, with a show of anxiety.

"No," replied the Emperor. "The fact is, old man, I - ah - I forgot to take the crown off when I went to bed."

Thus began that wonderful reign which forms so many dazzling pages in modern history. Bonaparte's first act after providing lucrative positions for his family was to write another letter, couched in language of a most fraternal nature, to the King of England, asking for peace.

"Dear Cousin George," he wrote, "you have probably read in the newspapers by this time that I'm working under a new alias, and I hope you will like it as well as I do. It's great fun, but there is one feature of it all that I don't like. I hate to be fighting with my new cousins all the time, and particularly with you whom I have always loved deeply, though secretly. Now, my dear George, let me ask you what's the use of a prolonged fight? You've waxed fat in ten years, and so have I. We've painted the earth red between us. Why can't we be satisfied? Why should our relations continue to be strained? I've got some personal relations I'd like to have strained, but I can attend to them myself. Let US have peace. I don't want too big a piece. Give me enough, and you can have the rest. Let us restore the entente cordiale and go about our business without any further scrapping. 'Let dogs delight to bark and bite,' as your illustrious poet hath it, 'for 'tis their nature to.' As for us, the earth is large enough for both. You take the Western Hemisphere and I'll keep this. Russia and the others can have what remains.

Yours truly,

NAPOLEON,
Emperor of the French.

"P.S. - I enclose a stamped and directed envelope for a reply, and if I don't get it inside of two weeks I'll come over and smoke you out."

To this peace-seeking communication England, through her ministers, replied to the effect that she wanted peace as much as France did, but that she could not enter into it without the consent of Russia.

"That settles it," said Napoleon. "It's to be war. I'm willing to divide creation with England, but two's company and three's a crowd, and the Russian Bear must keep his paws off. I will go to Italy, Bourrienne, collect a few more thrones, and then we'll get to work on a new map of Europe. Russia never did look well or graceful on the existing maps. It makes the continent look lop-sided, and Germany and Austria need trimming down a bit. I propose to shove Russia over into Asia, annex Germany and Austria to France, drop Turkey into the Bosporus, and tow England farther north and hitch her on to the north pole. Wire the Italians to get out their iron crown and dust it off. I'll take a run down to Milan, in May, and give my coronation performance there. Such a good show as that of December 2nd ought to be taken on the road."

The latter part of this plan was fulfilled to the letter, and on the 20th of May, 1805, Bonaparte and Josephine were crowned King and Queen of Italy at Milan.

"Now, my dear," said Bonaparte, after the ceremony, "hereafter we must drop the first person singular I and assume the dignity of the editorial WE. Emperors and editors alike are entitled to the distinction. It's a sign of plurality which is often quite as effective as a majority. Furthermore, you and We can do it logically, for we are several persons all at once, what with the assortment of thrones that we have acquired in the second-hand shops of the earth, all of which must be sat on."

Crowned King of Italy, leaving Eugene de Beauharnais as Viceroy at Milan, Napoleon returned to Paris.

"Now that We have replenished our stock of crowns," he said to his generals, "We will make a tour of Germany. We've always had a great desire to visit Berlin, and now's our imperial chance. Tell the arch-treasurer to telephone Frederick to reserve his best palace for our occupancy."

Then began a series of war-clouds which kept the European correspondents of the American Sunday newspapers in a state of anxious turmoil for years. In our own time a single war-cloud is enough to drive a capable correspondent to the verge of desperation, but when we consider that Bonaparte was letting loose the clouds of war in all sections of Europe simultaneously, it is easy to understand how it has come about that we of to-day, who study history in the daily press, have the most vague ideas as to the motives of the quarrelling potentates at the beginning of this century.

For instance, after starting for Berlin, Bonaparte makes a diversion at Ulm, and ends for the moment by capturing Vienna and taking up his abode in the castle of Schonbrunn, the home of the Austrian Caesars. Then the scene of activity is transferred to Cape Trafalgar, where Nelson routs the French fleet, and Bonaparte is for an instant discomfited, but above which he rises superior.

"If We had been there ourself We'd have felt worse about it," he said. "But We were not, and therefore it is none of our funeral - and, after all, what has it accomplished? The hoard of aldermen of London have named a square in London after the cape, and stuck up a monument to Nelson in the middle of it, which is the rendezvous of all the strikers and socialists of England. Some day We'll go over to Trafalgar Square ourself and put a new face on that statue, and it will bear some resemblance to us, unless We are mistaken. When We get back to Paris, likewise, We will issue an imperial decree ordering a new navy for these capable admirals of ours more suited to their abilities, and M. Villeneuve shall have his choice between a camel and a gravy-boat for his flag-ship."

Nevertheless, the Emperor realized that his prestige had received a blow which it was necessary to retrieve.

"Paris doesn't like it," wrote Fouche, "and the general sentiment seems to be that your show isn't what it used to be. You need a victory just about now, and if you could manage to lose a leg on the field of battle it would strengthen your standing with your subjects."

"Good Fouche," murmured the Emperor to himself as he read the despatch. "You are indeed watchful of our interests. It shall be done as you suggest, even if it costs a leg. We will engage the Russians at Austerlitz."

On the 2d of December this battle of the Emperors was fought, and resulted in a most glorious victory for the French arms.

"We scored seven touch-downs in the first five minutes, and at the end of the first half were ten goals to the good," said Bonaparte, writing home to Josephine, "and all without my touching the ball. The Emperor of Germany and the excessively smart Alexander of Russia sat on dead-head hill and watched the game with interest, but in spite of my repeated efforts to get them to do so, were utterly unwilling to cover my bets on the final result. The second half opened brilliantly. Murat made a flying wedge with our centre-rush, threw himself impetuously upon Kutusoff, the Russian half-back, pushed the enemy back beyond the goal posts, and the game was practically over. The emperors on dead-head hill gave it up then and there, and the championship of 1805 is ours. We understand England disputes this, but we are willing to play them on neutral ground at any time. They can beat us in aquatic sports, but given a good, hard, real-estate field, we can do them up whether Wellington plays or not."

"It was a glorious victory," wrote Fouche to the Emperor, "and it has had a great effect on Paris. You are called the Hinkey of your time, but I still think you erred in not losing that leg. Can't you work in another coronation somewhere? You haven't acquired a new throne in over six months, and the people are beginning to murmur."

Bonaparte's reply was immediate.

"Am too busy to go throne-hunting. Send my brother Joseph down to Naples as my agent. There's a crown there. Let him put it on, and tell Paris that he is my proxy. Joseph may not want to go because of the cholera scare, but tell him We wish it, and if he still demurs whisper the word 'Alp' in his ear. He'll go when he hears that word, particularly if you say it in that short, sharp, and decisive manner to which it so readily lends itself."

These instructions were carried out, and Paris was for the time being satisfied; but to clinch matters, as it were, the Emperor went still further, and married Eugene de Beauharnais to the daughter of the King of Bavaria, conferred a few choice principalities upon his sister Eliza, and, sending for Prince Borghese, one of the most aristocratic gentlemen of Italy, gave him in marriage to his sister Pauline.

"We're getting into good society by degrees," wrote the Emperor to the Empress, "and now that you are the mother-in-law of a real prince, kindly see that your manner is imperious to the extreme degree, and stop serving pie at state banquets."

The succeeding two years were but repetitions of the first year of the Empire. Bonaparte proceeded from one victory to another. Prussia was humbled. The French Emperor occupied Berlin, and, as he had done in Italy, levied upon the art treasures of that city for the enrichment of Paris.

"We'll have quite a Salon if we go on," said Bonaparte.

"Anybody'd think you were getting up a corner in oil," said Frederick, ruefully, as he watched the packers at work boxing his most treasured paintings for shipment.

"We am getting up a corner in all things," retorted Bonaparte. "Paris will soon be the Boston of Europe - it will be the Hub of the Universe."

"You might leave me something," said the Prussian king. "I haven't an old master left."

"Well, never mind," said Napoleon, soothingly. "We'll be a young master to you. Now go to bed, like a good fellow, and take a good rest. There's a delegation of Poles waiting for me outside. They think We am going to erect a telegraph system to Russia, and they want employment."

"As operators?" asked Frederick, sadly.

"No, stupid," returned Napoleon, "as Poles."

The Prussian left the room in tears. To his great regret policy compelled Bonaparte to decline the petition of the Polanders to be allowed to rehabilitate themselves as a nation. As we have seen, he was a man of peace, and many miles away from home at that, and hence had no desire to further exasperate Russia by meddling in an affair so close to the Czar's heart. This diplomatic foresight resulted in the Peace of Tilsit. The Czar, appreciating Bonaparte's delicacy in the matter of Poland, was quite won over, and consented to an interview by means of which a basis might be reached upon which all might rest from warfare. Tilsit was chosen as the place of meeting, and fearing lest they might be interrupted by reporters, the two emperors decided to hold their conference upon a raft anchored in the middle of the river Niemen. It must be remembered that tugs had not been invented at this time, so that the raft was comparatively safe from those "Boswells of the news," as reporters have been called. Fouche was very anxious about this decision however.

"Look out for yourself, my dear Emperor," he wrote. "Wear a cork suit, or insist that the raft shall be plentifully supplied with life-preservers. Those Eastern emperors would like nothing better than to have you founder in the Niemen."

"We are not afraid," Napoleon replied. "If the craft sinks We shall swim ashore on Alexander's back." Nevertheless, all other historians to the contrary, Bonaparte did wear a cork suit beneath his uniform. We have this on the authority of the nephew of the valet of the late Napoleon III., who had access to the private papers of this wonderful family.

Nothing disastrous occurred upon this occasion in spite of the temptation thrown in Alexander's way to sink the raft and thus rid the world of a dangerous rival to his supremacy. The conference resulted in a treaty of peace, concluded on the 7th of July, 1807, and by it a few more thrones were added to the Bonaparte collection. Jerome, who had been trying to make a living as a music teacher in America, having been divorced from his American wife and married to another, was made King of Westphalia.

"Having made a failure in the West, my dear brother," said Bonaparte, "what could be more appropriate?"

Louis was made King of Holland, and Joseph's kingship of Naples was fully recognized, and, further, Bonaparte was enabled to return to Paris and show himself to the citizens of that fickle city, who were getting restive under Josephine's rule.

"They like Josephine well enough," wrote Fouche, "but the men prefer to have you here. The fact that things run smoothly under a woman's rule is giving the female suffragists a great boom, and the men say that domestic life is being ruined.

Cooks are scarce, having deserted the kitchen for the primaries, and altogether the outlook is effeminate. Therefore, come back as soon as you can, for if you don't the first thing we know the women will be voting, and you'll find you'll have to give up your seat to a lady."

The Emperor's return to Paris was marked by great rejoicing, particularly by the large number of hatters and laundresses and stable-boys whom he had in the meantime paid for their early services by making them dukes and duchesses. The court was magnificent, and entirely new. No second-hand nobles were allowed within the sacred circle, and the result was one of extreme splendor. In a small way, to maintain the interest which he had inspired, as well as to keep up the discipline of his army, a few conquests, including those of Spain and Portugal, were indulged in. Joseph was removed from a comfortable, warm throne at Naples and made King of Spain, and Murat was substituted for him at Naples. The Emperor's elder brother did not like the change, but submitted as gracefully as ever.

"Naples was extremely comfortable," he said, "but this Madrid position is not at all to my taste. I prefer macaroni to garlic, and I cannot endure these Carmencita dances - they remind me too much of the green-apple season in the old Corsican days. However, what my brother wills I do, merely from force of habit - not that I fear him or consider myself bound to obey him, mind you, but because I am averse to family differences. One must yield, and I have always been the self-sacrificing member of the family. He's put me here, and I hope to remain."

This promotion of Joseph was a misstep for one who desired peace, and Bonaparte soon found another war with Austria on the tapis because of it. Emperor Francis Joseph, jealous perhaps of the copyright on his name, declined to recognize King Joseph of Spain. Whereupon Bonaparte again set out for Austria, where, on the 6th of July, 1809, Austria having recognized the strength of Bonaparte's arguments, backed up, as they were, by an overwhelming force of men, each worthy of a marshal's baton, and all confident, under the new regime, of some day securing it, an armistice was agreed upon, and on the 14 th of October a treaty satisfactory to France was signed.

"If I have to come back again, my dear Emperor Joseph," Bonaparte said, as he set out for Paris, "it will be for the purpose of giving you a new position, which you may not like so well as the neat and rather gaudy sinecure you now hold."

"Which is -?" added the Austrian.

"I'll bring you a snow-shovel and set you to clearing off the steps."

"What steps?" queried the Austrian anxiously.

"The back-steppes of Russia," replied Napoleon, sternly. "The only thing that keeps me from doing it now is that I - ah - I hate to do anything unkind to the father of - ah - your daughter Marie-Louise, whom I met at the dance last night, and who, between you and me, looks remarkably like the only woman I ever loved."

CHAPTER X

THE FALL OF THE EMPIRE 1810-1814

Just before the opening of the year 1810, which marked the beginning of Bonaparte's decay, Fouche demanded an audience.

"Well, Fouche," said the Emperor, "what now?"

"This Empire can't go much further, Your Majesty, unless more novelty is introduced. I've had my men out all through France taking notes, and there's but one opinion among 'em all. You've got to do something new or stop the show. If you'd only done what I suggested at Austerlitz, and lost a leg, it would have been different. The people don't ask much song-and-dance business from a one-legged man."

"We compromised with you there," retorted Napoleon. "At Ratisbon our imperial foot was laid up for a week."

"Yes - but you didn't lose it," returned Fouche. "Can't you see the difference? If you'd lost it, and come home without it, there'd have been evidence of your suffering. As it is, do you know what your enemies are saying about your foot?"

"We do not," said the Emperor, sternly. "What do they say?"

"Well, the Bourbons say you stepped on it running away from the enemy's guns, and the extreme Republicans say your wound is nothing but gout and the result of high, undemocratic living. Now, my dear sir - Sire, I mean - I take a great deal of interest in this Empire. It pays me my salary, and I've had charge of the calcium lights for some time, and I don't want our lustre dimmed, but it will be dimmed unless, as I have already told you a million times, we introduce some new act on our programme. 1492 didn't succeed on its music, or its jokes, or its living pictures. It was the introduction of novelties every week that kept it on the boards for four hundred years."

"Well - what do you propose?" asked Bonaparte, recognizing the truth of Fouche's words.

"I - ah - I think you ought to get married," said Fouche.

"We am married, you - you - idiot," cried Bonaparte.

"Well, marry again," said Fouche. "You've been giving other people away at a great rate for several years - what's the matter with acquiring a real princess for yourself?"

"You advise bigamy, do you?" asked Bonaparte, scornfully.

"Not on your life," returned Fouche, "but a real elegant divorce, followed by an imperial wedding, would rattle the bones of this blasé old Paris as they haven't been rattled since Robespierre's day."

Bonaparte reddened, then, rising from the throne and putting his hand to the side of his mouth, he said, in a low, agitated tone:

"Close the door, Fouche. Close the door and come here. We want to whisper something to you."

The minister did as he was bidden.

"Fouche, old boy," chuckled the Emperor in the ear of his rascally aide - "Fouche, you're a mind-reader. We've been thinking of just that very thing for some time - in fact, ever since We met that old woman Emperor Francis Joseph. He'd make an elegant mother-in-law."

"Precisely," said Fouche. "His daughter Marie-Louise, an archduchess by birth, is the one I had selected for you. History will no doubt say that I oppose this match, and publicly perhaps I may seem to do so, but you will understand, my dear Sire, that this opposition will serve, as it is designed to serve, as an advertisement of our enterprise, and without advertising we might as well put up the shutters. Shall we - ah - announce the attraction to the public?"

"Not yet," said Napoleon. "We must get rid of our leading lady before we bring on the understudy."

It is a sad chapter in the history of this eminent man wherein is told the heart-breaking story of his sacrifice - the giving up through sheer love of his country of the only woman he had ever loved, and we should prefer to pass it over in silence. We allude to it here merely to show that it was brought about by the exigencies of his office, and that it was nothing short of heroic self-abnegation which led this faithful lover of his adopted native land to put the beautiful Josephine away from him. He had builded an Empire for an opera bouffe people, and he was resolved to maintain it at any cost.

In March, 1810, Bonaparte, having in his anxiety to spare the feelings of the divorced Josephine, wooed Marie-Louise by proxy in the person of Marshal Berthier, met his new fiancee at Soissons.

"It is three months since we lost our beloved Josephine," he said to Fouche, with tears in his voice, "but the wound is beginning to heal. We fear we shall never love again, but for the sake of the Empire we will now begin to take notice once more. We will meet our bride-elect at Soissons, and escort her to Paris ourself."

This was done, and on the 2nd of April, 1810, Marie-Louise became Empress of France. Josephine, meanwhile, had retired to Malmaison with alimony of 3,000,000 francs.

Fouche was delighted; Paris was provided with conversation enough for a year in any event, and Bonaparte found it possible to relax a little in his efforts to inspire interest. His main anxiety in the ensuing year was as to his family affairs. His brothers did not turn out so highly successful as professional kings as he had hoped, and it became necessary to depose Louis the King of Holland and place him under arrest. Joseph, too, desired to resign the Spanish throne, which he had found to be far from comfortable, and there was much else to restore Bonaparte's early proneness to irritability; nor was his lot rendered any more happy by Marie-Louise's expressed determination not to go to tea with Josephine at Malmaison on Sunday nights, as the Emperor wished her to do.

"You may go if you please," said she, "but I shall not. Family reunions are never agreeable, and the circumstances of this are so peculiar that even if they had redeeming features this one would be impossible."

"We call that rebellion - don't you?" asked Bonaparte of Fouche.

"No," said Fouche. "She's right, and it's for your good. If she and Josephine got chumming and compared notes, I'm rather of the opinion that there'd be another divorce."

Fouche's reply so enraged the Emperor that he dismissed him from his post, and the Empire began to fall.

"I leave you at your zenith, Sire," said Fouche. "You send me to Rome as governor in the hope that I will get the Roman fever and die. I know it well; but let me tell you that the reaction is nearly due, and with the loss of your stage manager the farce begins to pall. Farewell. If you can hook yourself on to your zenith and stay there, do so, but that you will I don't think."

It was as Fouche said. Perplexities now arose which bade fair to overwhelm the Emperor. For a moment they cleared away when the infant son of Marie-Louise and Bonaparte was born, but they broke out with increasing embarrassment immediately after.

"What has your son-in-law named his boy, Francis Joseph?" asked Alexander of Russia.

"King of Rome," returned the Austrian.

"What!" cried Alexander, "and not after you - or me? The coxcomb! I will make war upon him."

This anecdote is here given to the world for the first time. It is generally supposed that the rupture of friendly relations between Alexander and Bonaparte grew out of other causes, but the truth is as indicated in this story. Had Fouche been at hand, Bonaparte would never have made the mistake, but it was made, and war was declared.

After a succession of hard-fought battles the invading army of the Emperor entered Moscow, but Napoleon's spirit was broken.

"These Russian names are giving us paresis!" he cried. "How I ever got here I don't know, and I find myself unprovided with a return ticket. The names of the Russian generals, to say nothing of those of their rivers and cities, make my head ache, and have ruined my teeth. I fear, Davoust, that I have had my day. It was easy to call on the Pollylukes to surrender in Africa; it never unduly taxed my powers of enunciation to speak the honeyed names of Italy; the Austrian tongue never bothered me; but when I try to inspire my soldiers with remarks like, 'On to Smolensko!' or 'Down with Rostopchin!' and 'Shall we be discouraged because Tchigagoff, and Kutusoff, and Carrymeoffski, of the Upperjnavyk Cgold Sdream Gards, oppose us?' I want to lie down and die. What is the sense of these barbed-wire names, anyhow? Why, when I was told that Barclay de Tolly had abandoned Vitepsk, and was marching on Smolensko with a fair chance of uniting with Tormagoff and Wittgenstein, I was so mixed that I couldn't tell whether Vitepsk was a brigadier-general or a Russian summer-resort. Nevertheless, we have arrived, and I think we can pass a comfortable winter in Moscow. Is Moscow a cold place, do you know?"

Marshal Ney looked out of the window.

"No, Your Majesty," he said; "I judge from appearances that it's the hottest place in creation, just now. Look!"

Bonaparte's heart sank within him. He looked and saw the city in flames.

"Well," he cried, "why don't you do something? What kind of theatrical soldiers are you? Ring up the fire department! Ah, Fouche, Fouche, if you were only here now! You could at least arrest the flames."

It was too late. Nothing could be done, and the conquering hero of nearly twenty years now experienced the bitterness of defeat. Rushing through the blazing town, he ordered a retreat, and was soon sadly wending his way back to Paris.

"We are afraid," he murmured, "that that Moscow fire has cooked our imperial goose."

Then, finding the progress of the army too slow, and anxious to hear the news of Paris, Napoleon left his troops under the command of Ney and pushed rapidly on, travelling incognito, not being desirous of accepting such receptions and fetes in his honor as the enemy had in store for him.

"I do not like to leave my army in such sore straits," he said, "but I must. I am needed at the Tuileries. The King of Rome has fallen in love with his nurse, and I understand also that there is a conspiracy to steal the throne and sell it. This must not be. Reassure the army of my love. Tell them that they are, as was the army of Egypt, my children, and that they may play out in the snow a little while longer, but must come in before they catch cold."

With these words he was off. Paris, as usual, received him with open arms. Things had been dull during his absence, and his return meant excitement. The total loss of the French in this campaign was 450,000 men, nearly a thousand cannon, and seventy-five eagles and standards.

"It's a heavy loss," said the Emperor, "but it took a snow-storm to do it. I'd rather fight bears than blizzards; but the French must not be discouraged. Let them join the army. The Russians have captured three thousand and forty-eight officers whose places must be filled. If that isn't encouragement to join the army I expect to raise next spring I don't know what is. As for the eagles - you can get gold eagles in America for ten dollars apiece, so why repine! On with the dance, let joy be unconfined!"

It was too late, however. The Empire had palled. Bonaparte could have started a comic paper and still have failed to rouse Paris from its lethargy, and Paris is the heart of France. Storms gathered, war-clouds multiplied, the nations of the earth united against him, the King of Rome began cutting his teeth and destroyed the Emperor's rest. The foot-ball of fate that chance had kicked so high came down to earth with a sickening thud, and Mr. Bonaparte of Corsica yielded to the inevitable.

"Fouche," he said, sending for the exiled minister in his extremity, "when I lost you I lost my leading man - the star of my enterprise. During your absence the prompter's box has been empty, and I don't know what to do. The world is against me - even France. I see but one thing left. Do you think I could restore confidence by divorcing Marie-Louise and remarrying Josephine? It strikes me that an annual shaking-up of that nature would sort of liven matters up.

"No!" said Fouche, "it won't do. They've had one divorce. You mustn't repeat yourself now. You forget the thing I've always tried to impress upon you. Be New; not parvenu or ingenue, but plain up and down New is what you need to be. It would have been just the same if you'd thrashed Russia. They'd have forced you to go on and conquer China; then they'd have demanded a war with Japan, after which they'd have dethroned you if you didn't annex the Sandwich Islands to the United States, and then bag the whole thing for France. This is what you get for wanting to rule the French people. You can't keep quiet - you've got to have a move on you constantly or they won't have you. Furthermore, you mustn't make 'em laugh except at the other man. You've had luck in that respect, but there's no telling how long it will continue now that you have a son. He's beginning to say funny things, and they're generally at your expense, and one or two people hereabouts have snickered at you already."

"What do you mean?" said Napoleon, with a frown. "What has the boy said about me?"

"He told the Minister of Finance the other night that now that you were the father of a real Emperor's grandson, you had a valid claim to respectability, and he'd bite the head off the first person who said you hadn't," said Fouche.

"Well - that certainly was standing up for his daddy," said the Emperor, fondly.

"Ye-e-es," said Fouche, "but it's one of those double back-action remarks that do more harm than good."

"Well," said Bonaparte, desperately, "let the boy say what he pleases; he's my son, and he has that right. The thing for us to decide is, what shall we do now?"

"There are three things left," said Fouche.

"And they?" asked the Emperor.

"Write Trilby, abdicate, or commit suicide. The first is beyond you. You know enough about Paris, but your style is against you. As for the second, abdication - if you abdicate you may come back, and the trouble will begin all over again. If you commit suicide, you won't have any more rows. The French will be startled, and say that it's a splendid climax, and you will have the satisfaction of knowing that some other man will try to please them with the same result."

"It shall be abdication," said the Emperor, with a sigh. "I don't mind suicide, but, hang it, Fouche, if I killed myself I could not read what the papers said about it. As for writing Trilby, it would do more for royalty than for me. Therefore I will go to Fontainebleau and abdicate. I will go into exile at Elba. Exiles are most interesting people, and it may be that I'll have another chance."

This course was taken, and on the 20th of April, 1814, Bonaparte abdicated. His speech to his faithful guard was one of the most affecting farewells in history, and had much to do with the encore which Napoleon received less than a year after. Escorted by four commissioners, one from each of the great allied powers, Austria, Russia, England, and Prussia, and attended by a few attached friends and servants, Bonaparte set out from Paris. The party occupied fourteen carriages, Bonaparte in the first; and as they left the capital the ex-Emperor, leaning out of the window, looked back at the train of conveyances and sighed.

"What, Sire? You sigh?" cried Bertrand.

"Yes, Bertrand, yes. Not for my departed glory, but because I am a living Frenchman, and not a dead Irishman."

"And why so, Sire?" asked Bertrand.

"Because, my friend, of the carriages. There are fourteen in this funeral. Think, Bertrand," he moaned, in a tone rendered doubly impressive by the fact that it reminded one of Henry Irving in one of his most mannered moments. "Think how I should have enjoyed this moment had I been a dead Irishman!"

CHAPTER XI

ELBA - THE RETURN - WATERLOO - ST. HELENA 1814-1815

Bonaparte's spirits rose as the party proceeded. There were remarkable evidences all along the line of march that his greatness, while dimmed in one sense, had not diminished in others. A series of attacks upon him had been arranged, much to the fallen Emperor's delight.

"If you want to make a fellow popular, Bertrand," he remarked after one of them, "kick him when he's down. I'll wager I am having a better time now than Louis XVIII., and, after all, I regard this merely as a vacation. I'll have a good rest at Elba while Louis is pushing the button of government at Paris. After a while I'll come back and press the buttons and Louis will do the rest. There's some honey in the old Bees yet."

At Valence, however, the Emperor had a bitter cup to drain. Meeting Augereau there, with whom he had fallen out, he addressed him in his old-time imperial style, asking him what right he had to still live, and requesting him to stand out of his light. Augereau, taking advantage of the Emperor's fallen estate, replied in a spirited manner, calling Napoleon an ex-Emperor and a tin soldier, as well as applying several other epithets to his dethroned majesty which might be printed in a French book, but can have no place in this.

"We shall meet again," retorted Bonaparte, with a

threatening gesture.

"Not if I see you first," replied Augereau. "If we do, however, it will be under a new system of etiquette."

"I'll bet you a crown you'll be singing a new tune inside of a year," cried the exasperated Bonaparte.

"I'll go you," said Augereau, snapping his fingers. "Put up your crown."

Napoleon felt keenly the stinging satire of this retort. Bowing his head with a groan, he had to acknowledge that he had no crown, but in an instant he recovered.

"But I have a Napoleon left in my clothes!" he cried, with a dry laugh at his own wit. "I'll bet it against your income for the next forty centuries, which is giving you large odds, that I shall return, and when I do, Monsieur Augereau, your name will be Denis."

The appreciation of those about them of this sally so enraged Augereau that he was discomfited utterly, and he left Bonaparte's presence muttering words which are fortunately forgotten.

Arrived at Cannes, Bonaparte had his choice of vessels upon which to make his voyage to Elba, one English and one French. "I'll take the English. I shall not trust my life to a Bourbon ship if I know myself. I'd rather go to sea in a bowl," said he.

Hence it was that an English vessel, the Undaunted, had the honor of transporting the illustrious exile to his island dominion. On the 4th of May he landed, and immediately made a survey of his new kingdom.

"It isn't large," he observed, as he made a memorandum of its dimensions, "but neither is a canvas-back duck. I think we can make something of it, particularly as the people seem glad to see me."

This was indeed the truth. The Elbese were delighted to have Bonaparte in their midst. They realized that excursion steamers which had hitherto passed them by would now come crowded from main-top to keel with persons desirous of seeing the illustrious captive. Hotel rates rose 200 per cent., and on the first Sunday of his stay on the island the receipts of the Island Museum, as it was now called, were sufficient to pay its taxes to the French government, which had been in arrears for some time, ten times over.

"I feel like an ossified man or a turtle-boy," said the Emperor to Bertrand, as the curious visitors gaped awe-stricken at the caged lion. "If I only had a few pictures of myself to sell these people I could buy up the national debt, foreclose the mortgage, and go back to France as its absolute master."

The popularity of Bonaparte as an attraction to outsiders so endeared him to the hearts of his new subjects that he practically had greater sway here than he ever had in the palmy days of the Empire. The citizens made him master of everything, and Bonaparte filled the role to the full. Provided with guards and servants, he surrounded himself with all the gaud and glitter of a military despotism, and, in default of continents to capture, he kept his hand in trim as a commander by the conquest of such small neighboring islands as nature had placed within reach, but it could hardly be expected that he could long remain tranquil. His eyes soon wearied of the circumscribed limits of Elba.

"It's all very well to be monarch of all you survey, Bertrand," said he, mournfully, "but as for me, give me some of the things that can't be seen. I might as well be that old dried-up fig of a P. T. Olemy over there in Egypt as Emperor of a vest-pocket Empire like this. Isn't there any news from France?"

"Yes," returned Bertrand, "Paris is murmuring again. Louis

hasn't stopped eating yet, and the French think it's time his dinner was over."

"Ha!" cried Bonaparte in ecstasy. "I thought so. He's too much of a revivalist to suit Paris. Furthermore, I'm told he's brought out his shop-worn aristocracy to dazzle France again. They're all wool and a yard wide, but you needn't think my handmade nobility is going to efface itself just because the Montmorencies and the Rohans don't ask it out to dine. My dukes and duchesses will have something to say, I fancy, and if my old laundress, the Duchess of Dantzig, doesn't take the starch out of the old regime I'll be mightily mistaken."

And this was the exact situation. As Bonaparte said, the old regime by their hauteur so enraged the new regime that by the new year of 1815 it was seen by all except those in authority that the return of the exile, Corporal Violet, as he was now called, was inevitable. So it came about that on the 20th of February, his pockets stuffed with impromptu addresses to the people and the army, Bonaparte, eluding those whose duty it was to watch him, set sail, and on the 1st of March he reached Cannes, whence he immediately marched, gaining recruits at every step, to Paris.

At Lyons he began to issue his impromptu addresses, and they were in his best style.

"People of France," ran one, "I am refreshed, and have returned to resume business at the old stand. March 21st will be bargain day, and I have on hand a select assortment of second-hand goods. One king, one aristocracy, much worn and slightly dog-eared, and a monarchy will be disposed of at less than cost. Come early and avoid the rush. A dukedom will be given away with every purchase. Do not forget the address - The Tuileries, Paris."

This was signed "Napoleon, Emperor." Its effect was instantaneous, and the appointment was faithfully kept, for on the evening of March 20th the Emperor, amid great enthusiasm, entered the Tuileries, where he was met by all his old friends, including Fouche.

"Fouche," he said, as he entered the throne-room, "give my card to Louis the XVIII., and ask him if his luggage is ready. Make out his bill, and when he has paid it, tell him that I have ordered the 6:10 train to start at 9:48. He can easily catch it."

"He has already departed, Sire," returned Fouche. "He had an imperative engagement in the Netherlands. In his haste he left his crown hanging on the hat-rack in the hall."

"Well, send it to him," replied Bonaparte. "I don't want HIS crown. I want my own. It shall never be said that I robbed a poor fellow out of work of his hat."

Settled once more upon his imperial throne, the main question which had previously agitated the Emperor and his advisers, and particularly his stage-manager, Fouche, whom he now restored to his old office, came up once more. "What next?" and it was harder to answer than ever, for Bonaparte's mind was no longer alert. He was listless and given to delay, and, worst of all, invariably sleepy. It was evident that Elba had not proved as restful as had been hoped.

"You should not have returned," said Fouche, firmly. "America was the field for you. That's where all great actors go sooner or later, and they make fortunes. A season in New York would have made you a new man. As it is you are an old man. It seems to me that if an Irishman can leave Queenstown with nothing but his brogue and the clothes on his back and become an alderman of New York or Chicago inside of two years, you with all the advertising you've had ought to be able to get into Congress anyhow - you've got money enough for the Senate."

"But they are not my children, those Americans," remonstrated Napoleon, rubbing his eyes sleepily.

"Well, France isn't the family affair it once was, either," retorted Fouche, "and you'll find it out before long. However, we've got to do the best we can. Swear off your old ways and come out as a man of Peace. Flatter the English, and by all means don't ask your mother-in-law Francis Joseph to send back the only woman you ever loved. He's got her in Vienna, and he's going to keep her if he has to put her in a safe-deposit vault."

It would have been well for Napoleon had he heeded this advice, but as he walked about the Tuileries alone, and listened in vain for the King of Rome's demands for more candy, and failed to see that interesting infant sliding down the banisters and loading his toy cannons with his mother's face-powder, he was oppressed by a sense of loneliness, and could not resist the temptation to send for them.

"This will be the last chip I'll put on my shoulder, Fouche," he pleaded.

"Very well," returned Fouche. "Put it there, but I warn you. This last chip will break the Empire's back."

The demand was made upon Austria, and, as Fouche had said, the answer was a most decided refusal, and the result was war. Again the other powers allied against Napoleon. The forces of the enemy were placed under Wellington. Bonaparte led his own in person, buying a new uniform for the purpose. "We can handle them easily enough," said he, "if I can only keep awake. My situation at present reminds me so much of the old Bromide days that I fall asleep without knowing it by a mere association of ideas. Still, we'll whip 'em out of their boots."

"What boots?" demanded Fouche.

"Their Wellingtons and their Bluchers," retorted the Emperor, thereby showing that, sleepy as he was, he had not lost his old-time ability at repartee.

For once he was over-confident. He fought desperately and triumphantly for three or four days, but the fates held Waterloo in store. Routing the enemy at Ligny and Quatre Bras, he pushed on to where Wellington stood in Belgium, where, on the 18th of June, was fought the greatest of his battles.

"Now for the transformation scene," said Bonaparte on the eve of the battle. "If the weather is good we'll make these foreigners wish they had worn running-shoes instead of Wellingtons."

But the weather was not clear. It was excessively wet, and by nightfall Bonaparte realized that all was over. His troops were in fine condition, but the rain seemed to have put out the fires of the Commander's genius. As the Imperial Guard marched before him in review the Emperor gazed upon them fondly.

"They're like a picture!" he cried, enthusiastically. "Just see that line."

"Yes," returned Ney. "Very like a picture; they remind me in a way of a comic paper print, but that is more suitable for framing than for fighting."

The Emperor making no response, Ney looked up and observed that his Majesty had fallen asleep. "That settles it," he sighed. "To-day is the Waterloo of Napoleon Bonaparte. When a man sleeps at a moment like this his friends would better prepare for a wake."

And Ney was right. Waterloo was the Waterloo of Napoleon Bonaparte. The opposing armies met in conflict, and, as the world knows, the star of the great soldier was obscured forever, and France was conquered. Ruined in his fortunes, Bonaparte at once returned to Paris.

"Is there a steamer for New York to-night, Fouche?" he asked, as, completely worn out, he threw himself upon his throne and let his chin hang dejectedly over his collar.

"No, Sire," returned Fouche, with an ill-concealed chuckle. "There is not. You've missed your chance by two days. Then isn't another boat for ten days."

"Then I am lost," sobbed Napoleon.

"Yes, Sire, you are," returned Fouche. "Shall I offer a reward to anybody who will find you and return you in good order?"

"No," replied the Emperor. "I will give myself up."

"Wise man!" said Fouche, unsympathetically. "You're such a confounded riddle that I wonder you didn't do it long ago."

"Ah, Fouche!" sighed the Emperor, taking his crown out of his wardrobe and crushing it in his hands until the diamonds fell out upon the floor, "this shows the futility of making war without preparing for it by study. When I was a young man I was a student. I knew the pages of history by heart, and I learned my lessons well. While I was the student I was invincible. In mimic as in real war I was the conqueror. Everything I undertook came about as I had willed because I was the master of facts - I dealt in facts, and I made no mistakes. To-day I am a conquered man, and all because I have neglected to continue the study of the history of my people - of my adopted native land."

"Humph!" retorted Fouche. "I don't see how that would have helped matters any. All the history in creation could not have won the battle of Waterloo for you."

"Fool that you are!" cried Napoleon, desperately, rising. "Can't you see? Anybody who knows anything about the history of France knows that the battle of Waterloo resulted fatally for me. Had I known that, do you suppose I'd have gone there? Not I! I'd have gone fishing in the South of France instead, and this would not have happened. Leave me! I wish to

John Kendrick Bangs

be alone."

Left to his own reflections Bonaparte paced his room for hours. Then, tapping his bell, he summoned one of his faithful adherents.

"Monsieur le B-," he said, as the attendant entered, "you have heard the news?"

"Yes, Sire," sobbed Le B-.

"Do I not carry myself well in the hour of defeat?"

"You do, Your Majesty."

"Am I pale, Le B-?"

"No - no - oh, no, not at all, Sire."

"Tell me the truth, Le B-. We must not let the enemy find us broken when they arrive. How do I look? Out with it."

"Out of sight, Sire!" replied Le B-, bending backward as far as he could, and gazing directly at the ceiling.

"Then bring on your invader, and let us hear the worst," ordered Napoleon, encouraged by Le B-'s assurances.

A few days later, Bonaparte, having nothing else to do, once more abdicated, and threw himself upon the generosity of the English people.

"I was only fooling, anyhow," he said, with a sad smile. "If you hadn't sent me to Elba I wouldn't have come back. As for the fighting, you all said I was outside of the pale of civilization, and I had to fight. I didn't care much about getting back into the pail, but I really objected to having it said that I was in the tureen."

This jest completely won the hearts of the English who were used to just such humor, who loved it, and who, many years later, showed that love by the establishment of a comic journal as an asylum for bon-mots similarly afflicted. The result was, not death, but a new Empire, the Island of St. Helena.

"This," said Wellington, "will serve to make his jokes more far-fetched than ever; so that by sending him there we shall not only be gracious to a fallen foe, but add to the gayety of our nation."

CHAPTER XII

1815-1821-1895

It is with St. Helena that all biographies of Napoleon Bonaparte hitherto published have ended, and perhaps it is just as well that these entertaining works, prepared by purely finite minds, should end there. It is well for an historian not to tell more than he knows, a principle which has guided our pen from the inception of this work to this point, and which must continue to the bitter end. We shall be relentless and truthful to the last, even though in so doing we are compelled to overthrow all historical precedent.

Bonaparte arrived at St. Helena in October, 1815. He had embarked, every one supposed, with the impression that he was going to America, and those about him, fearing a passionate outbreak when he learned the truth, tried for a time to convince him that he had taken the wrong steamer; then when they found that he could not be deceived in this way, they made allusions to the steering-gear having got out of order, but the ex-Emperor merely smiled.

"You cannot fool me," he said. "I know whither I am drifting. I went to a clairvoyant before leaving Paris, who cast a few dozen horoscopes for me and they all ended at St. Helena. It is inevitable. I must go there, and all these fairy tales about wrong steamers and broken rudders and so on are useless. I submit. I could return if I wished, but I do not wish to return. By a mere speech to these sailors I could place myself in command of this ship to-day, turn her about and proclaim myself Emperor of the Seas; but I don't want to. I prefer dry land and peace to a coup de tar and the throne of Neptune."

All of which shows that the great warrior was weary.

Then followed a dreary exile of uneventful years, in which the ex-Emperor conducted paper campaigns of great fierceness against the English government, which with unprecedented parsimony allowed him no more than $60,000 a year and house rent.

"The idea of limiting me to five thousand dollars a month," he remarked, savagely, to Sir Hudson Lowe. "It's positively low."

"It strikes me as positively high," retorted the governor. "You know well enough that you couldn't spend ten dollars a week in this place if you put your whole mind on it, if you hadn't insisted on having French waiters in your dining-room, whom you have to tip every time they bring you anything."

"Humph!" said Bonaparte. "That isn't any argument. I'm a man used to handling large sums. It isn't that I want to spend money; it's that I want to have it about me in case of emergency. However, I know well enough why they keep my allowance down to $60,000."

"Why is it?" asked Sir Hudson.

"They know that you can't be bought for $60,000, but they wouldn't dare make it $60,000 and one cent," retorted the captive. "Put that in your cigarette and smoke it, Sir Harlem, and hereafter call me Emperor. That's my name, Emperor N. Bonaparte."

"And I beg that you will not call me Sir Harlem," returned the governor, irritated by the Emperor's manner. "My name is Hudson, not Harlem."

"Pray excuse the slip," said the Emperor, scornfully. "I knew you were named after some American river, I didn't know which. However, I imagined that the Harlem was nearer your size than the Hudson, since the latter has some pretensions to grandeur. Now please flow down to the sea and lose yourself, I'm getting sleepy again."

So, in constant conflict with Sir Hudson, who refused to call him by his title, and whom in consequence he refused to call by his proper name, answering such epithets as "Corporal" and "Major" with a savagely-spoken "Delaware" or an ironically respectful "Mohawk," Bonaparte dwelt at St. Helena until the 5th of May, 1821, when, historians tell us, he died. This is an error, for upon that date Bonaparte escaped. He had fought death too many times to succumb to him now, and, while the writers of history have in a sense stated the truth when they say that he passed away in the night, their readers have gained a false impression. It is the fact that Napoleon Bonaparte, like Dante and Virgil, passed over the dark river Styx as the honored leader of the rebellious forces of Hades. He did pass away in the night, but he went as he went from Elba, and, as we shall see, with more successful results.

For years the Government of Erebus had been unsatisfactory to many of its subjects, mainly on account of the arbitrary methods of the Weather Department.

"We are in a perpetual broil here," Caesar had said, "and I for one am getting tired of it. The country demands a change. This administration doesn't give us anything but dog-days."

For this the Roman warrior had been arrested and kept in an oven at the rear of the Erebian Tuileries, as Apollyon's Palace was called, for two centuries.

"The next rebel gets a gridiron, and the third will be served to Cerberus en brochette," cried Apollyon.

Thus matters had gone on for five or six hundred years, and no one had ventured to complain further, particularly in view of Caesar's comments upon the horrid details of his incarceration published several years after his release, under the title of "Two Centuries in an Oven; or, Four Thousand and Six in the Shade."

At the end of the eighteenth century, however, the aspect of affairs had changed. Apollyon had spent a great deal of his time abroad, and had failed to note how the revolution in America, the Reign of Terror in France, and the subsequent wars in Europe had materially increased the forces of the Republican Party in Hades. The French arrivals alone should have been sufficient to convince Apollyon that his attention to domestic affairs was needed, and that the Americanization of his domain was gaining a most considerable headway. All the movement really needed was a leader, but there was none to lead.

"Caesar's book has made us timid. I don't want any of it," said Alcibiades.

"I've had enough of public life," said Charlemagne.

"It's hot enough for us as it is," said all four of the "Three Musketeers."

"We'll have to get somebody who is not aware of the possibilities of our climate," observed Frederick the Great.

"Try Napoleon Bonaparte," suggested Louis XIV., with a chuckle, feeling that here was an opportunity to do one of two things, to get even with Apollyon, or, in case of the failure of the rebellion, to be revenged upon Bonaparte for his treatment of the Bourbons by securing for him the warmest reception the Kingdom of Hades could afford.

The suggestion, according to documents at hand which seem to be veracious, was adopted with enthusiasm. The exile was communicated with, and joy settled upon the people of Hades when word was received that Bonaparte was on his way. As we have seen, on the night of the 5th of May he left St. Helena, and on the 10th he landed on the right bank of the Styx. A magnificent army awaited him. To the Old Guard, many of whom had preceded him, was accorded the position of honor, and as Bonaparte stepped ashore the roof of Erebus was rent with vivas. Such a scene has never been witnessed before, and may never be witnessed again. The populace flocked about him, and strove to kiss his hand; some went so far as to clip off samples of his uniform to treasure in their homes. It was evident that the government must look to itself.

"What is this noise?" asked Apollyon, who had returned to his domain only the night before.

"Bonaparte has arrived," returned the head Imp, "and the people are in revolt."

Apollyon paled and summoned his ministers.

Meanwhile Bonaparte had held a council of war, appointing Caesar, Pompey, Alcibiades, and Charlemagne marshals of Hades.

"The first thing to be done is to capture the coal-yards," he said, taking in the situation at a glance. "Caesar, let the coal-yards be your care. Alcibiades will take the Three Musketeers, and by night will make a detour to the other side of the palace and open the sluices of the vitriol reservoir, which I understand run into the Styx. Pompey will surprise the stokers in the national engine-room with a force of ten thousand, put out the fires, and await further orders. Charlemagne will accompany me with the army to the palace, where I shall demand an audience with the king."

It will be seen at once that, granting the success of all these manoeuvres, Apollyon could not possibly hold out. As the Hollanders had only water with which to flood their country and rout their enemies, so Apollyon had only fire with which to wither an invader or a rebellious force. The quick mind of Bonaparte took this in on the instant. He was no longer listless and sleepy, for here was the grandest opportunity of his life, and he knew it.

Fortune favored him. In Hades fortune was a material personality, and not an abstract idea as she is with us, and when she met Bonaparte on his triumphal march along the Styx, she yielded to that fascination which even phlegmatic Englishmen could not deny that he possessed; and when at this meeting the man of the hour took her by the hand and breathed softly into her ear that she was in very truth the only woman he had ever loved, she instinctively felt that he had at last spoken from his heart of hearts.

"I believe you, Bonaparte," she murmured softly, "and I think I have shown you in the past that I am not indifferent to you. I am with you - Apollyon is doomed."

Thus encouraged, Bonaparte, followed by his constantly growing army, proceeded to the palace.

Apollyon received him with dignity.

"I am glad to receive so distinguished a person," he said.

"Thank you," said Bonaparte, "but this is not a society function, Your Highness - I have come here on business, so spare me your flatteries."

Apollyon turned purple with rage.

"Insolent!" he cried. "Consider yourself under arrest."

"Certainly," said Bonaparte, calmly. "Will you kindly hand me your crown?"

Apollyon rose in his wrath, and ordered his aides to arrest Bonaparte, and to cast him into the furnace. "Make it a million degrees Farenheit," he roared.

"I regret to inform your majesty," said the chief aide, "that word has just been received that the fires are out, the coal-yard has been captured by the rebels, and five adventurous spirits have let all the vitriol out of the reservoir into the Styx."

"Summon my guards, and have this man boned, then!" raged Apollyon.

"It is also with regret that I have to tell you," returned the aide, "that the Royal Guard has gone over to the enemy, having been promised higher wages."

"We have Cerberus left," cried Apollyon, "let him take this base intruder and tear him limb from limb."

Napoleon burst out into a laugh. "You will excuse me, Your Majesty," he said. "But Cerberus is already fixed. We poisoned two of his heads, and he is even now whining for his life with the third."

"Then am I undone," moaned Apollyon, covering his face with his hands.

"You are," said Bonaparte, "but we'll tie you up again in short order. We'll put you on one of your own gridirons and do you to a turn."

Of course this was the end.

In three days Napoleon had made himself master of the kingdom, had proclaimed the Empire with himself at its head. Apollyon was treated with consideration. His life was spared, but he was shorn of his power. Bonaparte sent him into exile at Paris, where, according to report, he still lives.

"Now for a new coronation," said the victor. "Send for the pope."

"Not this tune!" cried Caesar with a laugh. "The popes have always studiously avoided this place."

"Then," said Napoleon with a smile, "let Fortune crown me. After all, it has always been she who did it - why not now?"

Hence it was that at the dawning of New Year's day of 1822, Napoleon Bonaparte opened a new and most highly successful career. His power has increased day by day until now, when there is evidence that he has the greater part of the world in his firm grasp.

Some years later his beloved Bourrienne arrived.

"Remember, Bourrienne," he said, as he installed his old and faithful secretary in his new office, "you have always written my autographs for me, and shall still continue to do so, only please note the change. It is no longer Bonaparte, or Napoleon, Emperor of the French, it has become Napollyon, Emperor of Hades."

And to Fouche, when that worthy arrived, he said:

"Fouche, this is different from the old show. That original Empire of mine was ruined by just one thing. I was eternally anxious to provide for the succession, and out of that grew all my troubles; but here, as the little girl said about the apple-core, there ain't a-goin' to be no succession. I am here to stay. Meanwhile, Fouche, I have an impression that you and Augureau took more pleasure out of my misfortunes than I did; wherefore I authorize you to send for Augereau and take him swimming in the vitriol tank. It will do you both good."

As for Joseph, when he heard of his brother's new acquisition he reformed at once, led an irreproachable life in America, whither he had fled, and when he died went to the other place.

FOOTNOTE

{1} Napoleon's English at this time was not of the best quality

Choose from Thousands of 1stWorldLibrary Classics By

Ada Leverson
Adolphus William Ward
Aesop
Agatha Christie
Alexander Aaronsohn
Alexander Kielland
Alexandre Dumas
Alfred Gatty
Alfred Ollivant
Alice Duer Miller
Alice Turner Curtis
Alice Dunbar
Ambrose Bierce
Amelia E. Barr
Andrew Lang
Andrew McFarland Davis
Andy Adams
Anna Sewell
Annie Besant
Annie Hamilton Donnell
Annie Payson Call
Annonaymous
Anton Chekhov
Arnold Bennett
Arthur Conan Doyle
Arthur M. Winfield
Arthur Ransome
Atticus
B.H. Baden-Powell
B. M. Bower
Baroness Emmuska Orczy
Baroness Orczy
Basil King
Bayard Taylor
Ben Macomber
Bertha Muzzy Bower
Bjornstjerne Bjornson
Booth Tarkington
Boyd Cable
Bram Stoker
C. Collodi
C. E. Orr
C. M. Ingleby
Carolyn Wells
Catherine Parr Traill
Charles A. Eastman
Charles Dickens
Charles Dudley Warner
Charles Farrar Browne

Charles Ives
Charles Kingsley
Charles Klein
Charles Lathrop Pack
Charles Whibley
Charles Willing Beale
Charlotte M. Braeme
Charlotte M. Yonge
Charlotte Perkins Stetson
Clair W. Hayes
Clarence Day Jr.
Clarence E. Mulford
Clemence Housman
Confucius
Cornelis DeWitt Wilcox
Cyril Burleigh
D. H. Lawrence
Daniel Defoe
David Garnett
Don Carlos Janes
Donald Keyhoe
Dorothy Kilner
Dougan Clark
Douglas Fairbanks
E. Nesbit
E.P.Roe
E. Phillips Oppenheim
Edgar Rice Burroughs
Edith Van Dyne
Edith Wharton
Edward J. O'Biren
Edward S. Ellis
Edwin L. Arnold
Eleanor Atkins
Eliot Gregory
Elizabeth Gaskell
Elizabeth McCracken
Elizabeth Von Arnim
Ellem Key
Emerson Hough
Emily Dickinson
Enid Bagnold
Enilor Macartney Lane
Erasmus W. Jones
Ernie Howard Pie
Ethel Turner
Ethel Watts Mumford
Eugenie Foa
Eugene Wood

Evelyn Everett-green
Everard Cotes
F. H. Cheley
F. J. Cross
Federick Austin Ogg
Ferdinand Ossendowski
Francis Bacon
Francis Darwin
Frances Hodgson Burnett
Frances Parkinson Keyes
Frank Gee Patchin
Frank Harris
Frank Jewett Mather
Frank L. Packard
Frank V. Webster
Frederic Stewart Isham
Frederick Trevor Hill
Frederick Winslow Taylor
Friedrich Kerst
Friedrich Nietzsche
Fyodor Dostoyevsky
G.A. Henty
G.K. Chesterton
Gabrielle E. Jackson
Garrett P. Serviss
Gaston Leroux
George Ade
Geroge Bernard Shaw
George Durston
George Ebers
George Eliot
George MacDonald
George Meredith
George Orwell
George Tucker
George W. Cable
George Wharton James
Gertrude Atherton
Grace E. King
Grace Gallatin
Grant Allen
Guillermo A. Sherwell
Gulielma Zollinger
Gustav Flaubert
H. A. Cody
H. B. Irving
H.C. Bailey
H. G. Wells
H. H. Munro

H. Irving Hancock
H. Rider Haggard
H. W. C. Davis
Hamilton Wright Mabie
Hans Christian Andersen
Harold Avery
Harold McGrath
Harriet Beecher Stowe
Harry Houidini
Helent Hunt Jackson
Helen Nicolay
Hendrik Conscience
Hendy David Thoreau
Henri Barbusse
Henrik Ibsen
Henry Adams
Henry Ford
Henry Frost
Henry James
Henry Jones Ford
Henry Seton Merriman
Henry W Longfellow
Herbert A. Giles
Herbert N. Casson
Herman Hesse
Homer
Honore De Balzac
Horace Walpole
Horatio Alger Jr.
Howard Pyle
Howard R. Garis
Hugh Lofting
Hugh Walpole
Humphry Ward
Ian Maclaren
Inez Haynes Gillmore
Irving Bacheller
Israel Abrahams
Ivan Turgenev
J.G.Austin
J. Henri Fabre
J. M. Barrie
J. Macdonald Oxley
J. S. Fletcher
J. S. Knowles
J. Storer Clouston
Jack London
Jacob Abbott
James Allen
James Andrews
James Baldwin

James DeMille
James Joyce
James Lane Allen
James Lane Allen
James Oliver Curwood
James Oppenheim
James Otis
James R. Driscoll
Jane Austen
Jens Peter Jacobsen
Jerome K. Jerome
John Burroughs
John Cournos
John F. Kennedy
John Gay
John Glasworthy
John Habberton
John Joy Bell
John Kendrick Bangs
John Milton
John Philip Sousa
Jonas Lauritz Idemil Lie
Jonathan Swift
Joseph A. Altsheler
Joseph Carey
Joseph Conrad
Joseph E. Badger Jr
Joseph Hergesheimer
Joseph Jacobs
Julian Hawthrone
Julies Vernes
Justin Huntly McCarthy
Kakuzo Okakura
Kenneth Grahame
Kenneth McGaffey
Kate Langley Bosher
Kate Langley Bosher
Katherine Cecil Thurston
Katherine Stokes
L. A. Abbot
L. T. Meade
L. Frank Baum
Latta Griswold
Laura Lee Hope
Laurence Housman
Leo Tolstoy
Leonid Andreyev
Lewis Carroll
Lilian Bell
Lloyd Osbourne
Louis Tracy

Louisa May Alcott
Lucy Fitch Perkins
Lucy Maud Montgomery
Lydia Miller Middleton
Lyndon Orr
M. Corvus
M. H. Adams
Margaret E. Sangster
Margaret Vandercook
Margret Penrose
Maria Edgeworth
Maria Thompson Daviess
Mariano Azuela
Marion Polk Angellotti
Mark Overton
Mark Twain
Mary Austin
Mary Catherine Crowley
Mary Cole
Mary Hastings Bradley
Mary Roberts Rinehart
Mary Rowlandson
M. Wollstonecraft Shelley
Maud Lindsay
Max Beerbohm
Myra Kelly
Nathaniel Hawthrone
Nicolo Machiavelli
O. F. Walton
Oscar Wilde
Owen Johnson
P.G. Wodehouse
Paul and Mabel Thorne
Paul G. Tomlinson
Paul Severing
Percy Brebner
Peter B. Kyne
Plato
R. Derby Holmes
R. L. Stevenson
R. S. Ball
Rabindranath Tagore
Rahul Alvares
Ralph Henry Barbour
Ralph Waldo Emmerson
Rene Descartes
Rex Beach
Rex E. Beach
Richard Harding Davis
Richard Jefferies
Richard Le Gallienne

Robert Barr
Robert Frost
Robert Gordon Anderson
Robert L. Drake
Robert Lansing
Robert Lynd
Robert Michael Ballantyne
Robert W. Chambers
Rosa Nouchette Carey
Rudyard Kipling
Samuel B. Allison
Samuel Hopkins Adams
Sarah Bernhardt
Selma Lagerlof
Sherwood Anderson
Sigmund Freud
Standish O'Grady
Stanley Weyman
Stella Benson
Stephen Crane
Stewart Edward White
Stijn Streuvels
Swami Abhedananda

Swami Parmananda
T. S. Ackland
T. S. Arthur
The Princess Der Ling
Thomas A. Janvier
Thomas A Kempis
Thomas Anderton
Thomas Bailey Aldrich
Thomas Bulfinch
Thomas De Quincey
Thomas H. Huxley
Thomas Hardy
Thomas More
Thornton W. Burgess
U. S. Grant
Valentine Williams
Various Authors
Victor Appleton
Virginia Woolf
Walter Camp
Walter Scott
Washington Irving
Wilbur Lawton

Wilkie Collins
Willa Cather
Willard F. Baker
William Dean Howells
William le Queux
W. Makepeace Thackeray
William W. Walter
Winston Churchill
Yei Theodora Ozaki
Yogi Ramacharaka
Young E. Allison
Zane Grey

www.ingramcontent.com/pod-product-compliance
Lightning Source LLC
Chambersburg PA
CBHW032008040426
42448CB00006B/542